The Creative Loop

How the Brain Makes a Mind

Also by Erich Harth

Windows on the Mind:
Reflections on the Physical Basis of Consciousness

Dawn of a Millennium: Beyond Evolution and Culture

The Creative Loop

How the Brain Makes a Mind

Erich Harth

A William Patrick Book

ADDISON-WESLEY PUBLISHING COMPANY

Reading, Massachusetts · Menlo Park, California · New York
Don Mills, Ontario · Wokingham, England · Amsterdam · Bonn
Sidney · Singapore · Tokyo · Madrid · San Juan
Paris · Seoul · Milan · Mexico City · Taipei

Excerpts from "The Universe" and "The Watch" by May Swenson reprinted by permission of The Literary Estate of May Swenson.

Excerpt from the "The Idea of Order at Key West" from *Collected Poems* by Wallace Stevens. Copyright 1936 by Wallace Stevens and renewed 1964 by Holly Stevens. Reprinted by permission of Alfred A. Knopf, Inc.

Excerpt from "Flux" by Theodore Melnechuk reprinted by permission of the author.

Illustration credits: p. xxiv — Photograph of Hindsgavl dagger reprinted by permission of Nationalmuseet, Kopenhagen; p. 69 — "St. Helena," from *The Senses*, Barlow and Mollon (eds.), reprinted by permission of Cambridge University Press; p. 81 — *The Innocent Eye Test* by Mark Tansey reprinted by permission of the Metropolitan Museum of Art, New York; pp. 54, 98, 138, 143, and 175 — drawings by Elaine de la Mata; pp. 51, 55, 64, 65, 91, 127, 139, 152, 153, and 177 — graphics by Ronald P. Bouverat.

Library of Congress Cataloging-in-Publication Data

Harth, Erich.
  The creative loop; how the brain makes a mind / Erich Harth.
    p.   cm.
  Includes bibliographical references and index.
  ISBN 0-201-57079-3
  1. Brain. 2. Mind and body. 3. Mind-brain identity theory.
4. Biophysics. I. Title.
QP360.H34   1993
612.8'2--dc20   93-22829
                                                                    CIP

Jacket design by Jean Seal
Jacket art by Lance Hidy
Text design by Wilson Graphics & Design (Kenneth J. Wilson)
Set in 10-point New Century Schoolbook by CopyRight, Inc.

1 2 3 4 5 6 7 8 9-MA-96959493
First printing, July 1993

for
Dorothy
with gratitude
and love

Contents

Preface

It was my intention to write another book on the brain. I have been intrigued with this organ for over a quarter of a century, and although I have studied its structure and function, and written about it in professional journals and in one book-length work for the general reader, I find myself as mystified as ever by the unique position it occupies for me in the universe. I am referring in particular to *my* brain, but I presume your brain occupies a similar position for you.

In thinking about this venture, I became more and more tempted to go beyond a description of how the brain helps me navigate through life, or what the underlying brain mechanisms are, and to give rein to the whole gamut of existential puzzlements that revolve around the two entities—myself on one side and the rest of the universe on the other—that interact through this three pounds of neural mass. I probably should have stifled the impulse, but the physicist in me becomes impatient when the talk is confined to neuroscience, and the neuroscientist in me grows restless when it is all about physics. In one sense, this book is to reconcile the two realms.

I believe that the questions that trouble me most are also the most puzzling to others. They become even more irksome when I try to define them for the purpose of telling the reader what is in store. To talk about ''my place vis-à-vis the universe'' must seem a hopelessly presumptuous, even arrogant, undertaking. But the brain that looks both in and out cannot help wondering at the strange duality of the world in which there is an *I* and an *it*, and the knowledge that in a matter of years, decades at most, there will be only *it*. We humans all share this predicament and face it in different ways.

In trying to assess the nature of my existence I came to examine a number of related puzzles. I believe that a juxtaposition of cosmic and biological evolution can help delineate our position in the universe, and that we may gain a better fix on the human mind by comparing our brains with our computers, and by looking at our electronic robots alongside the clockwork puppets that so intrigued our ancestors two centuries ago.

Here I must confess to a profound dilemma. I wish I could unequivocally believe in a soul, because it would explain so much that is mysterious about human existence. I can't, and I am not even flirting with the idea. I also wish I could subscribe to orthodox materialism, to take the veil off the mystery of the mind-brain, and to convince you that all the wondrous peregrinations of your conscious mind not only can be understood as the workings of a complex machinery of neural switches and relays, but also can be translated, duplicated, even improved, by machinery of our design and making.

Unfortunately, I see materialism as an outdated concept, rooted in the nineteenth-century belief that all phenomena in the world could be explained as the mechanical interactions between many small indivisible and permanent material objects or *elementary particles*. Since then, the world of these supposedly indestructible units has been opened to reveal an immaterial confusion of fields, virtual states, and questionable causal relations. In a most unexpected development, this world of the ultrasmall has been linked recently to questions concerning the opposite end of the cosmic scale, the birth and evolution of the universe at large.[1] A *materialist* explanation may be appropriate for an understanding of the workings of a steam engine or even of a computer chip, but may miss the mark when we try to understand what makes us think. I would favor a *physicalist* approach, by which I mean the working assumption that the broad field of *physics* ultimately must account for most things we observe, including our own minds. This differs fundamentally from orthodox materialism because it leaves the door open to the unknown laws and relations of a yet to be explored territory.

The fields of physics and neuroscience have grown into formidable structures whose languages are all but impenetrable to the uninitiated. But when we come to questions concerning the workings of the mind, we find that the thicket of technical jargon only hides our profound ignorance, and that simple language has a better chance of cutting through some of the underbrush. We must come out into the open again and speak clearly, that is, simply. This I will try to do.

The questions raised will, I hope, be more important than the few answers I may provide. The brain is still to be the centerpiece of our discussions. How, I will ask, does it create its world of images, and how does that world compare with the corresponding *real* objects and events? What role do time and space play in the image world, the world of the mind? Is there anything at all we can say about consciousness? What is sensation? What are intentionality, creativity?

In discussing the brain I will pay particular attention to a peculiar feature of brain structure that all too often is overlooked: the existence, the ubiquity, of feedback loops. This means that what is received at any one brain level depends on what goes on at that same level, and what is sent to the next level depends on things happening at that next level. The mechanism is one of *self-reference*. I will propose ways in which these self-referent loops contribute to some of the qualities we associate with the human mind: consciousness, creativity.

I use the word *contribute* to express my belief that these mechanisms are necessary in the making of a mind. But they are not the whole story; otherwise we could build a robot tomorrow, using these same principles, and expect it to be conscious and creative.

But perhaps we are taking too much for granted. It has been suggested that consciousness may be an artifact, and that creativity, intentionality, and selfhood are illusions. Why couldn't I be replaced by a machine? Would it, *should* it, matter to me? How human can a robot be, and to what extent do humans act like puppets? Are humans disappearing from the scene, being displaced by their own more intelligent creations?

These are complex questions, and some material from various sciences will be introduced in a nontechnical way as background material, but the important discussions are of such a nature that the simplest language is as expedient as the most abstruse. By aiming for the former, I hope that a broad audience will be able to participate in this adventure.

I owe a great debt to my family for helpful criticism and support, to my students at Syracuse University who collaborated on many ideas expressed here, to Lee Smolin and K. P. Unnikrishman for many helpful comments on the manuscript, and to my editor, William Patrick, without whose guidance this would have been a lesser work.

Introduction

What
is it about
the universe,
the universe about us stretching out?
We, within our brains,
within it,
think
we must unspin it.

From *The Universe*, May Swenson

The human body is an exquisite machine, the end product of several billion years of biological evolution. We have learned to understand much of the intricate structure and function of its various parts, including those of the most complex organ of all: the human brain. But some brain functions have stubbornly eluded our attempts at reducing them to the kind of mechanistic principles that allow us to understand an organ such as the heart.

The functions we are at a loss to explain all seem to emanate from, or pertain to, a *person*, an *I*, a *subject* who not only sees and hears but *perceives* what he or she sees and hears, who recalls and projects, associates, imagines, invents, creates. He or she also *feels*—is happy or sad, hopeful or despairing, elated or depressed, angry or in love. All of these functions, and many more, are subsumed collectively under the heading the *mind of man*.[1]

They all have in common the fact that nobody has yet succeeded in explaining them as chains of logical steps or mechanistic events. Niels Bohr was aware of that when he admonished a student with "You are not thinking, you are just being logical." Unable to conceive of a way of reducing mind functions to body functions, René Descartes (1596–1650) proposed a *dualist* model of man: a mechanistic body and a mind, or *soul*, made of different stuff and subject to different laws. The two touched and interacted at a single point in the brain, the pineal gland, but otherwise carried out their functions independently of one another.

The reason Descartes's name still figures so prominently in discussions of the mind-brain dilemma is that the matter simply has not been resolved. Many schools of thought have arisen in the past 350 years. Many *isms* have been defined and written about extensively. But it is not an overstatement when I say that in all this time there has not been a true advance in the subject matter, if by advance we mean the acquisition of an understanding that is generally agreed on by the experts in the field. Certainly, no such agreement exists, not among philosophers and not among workers in the various branches of neuroscience. Dualists of more or less Cartesian persuasion still exist in all these groups. Like Descartes, they maintain that mind requires something beyond the neural machinery of our brain.

Different varieties of *materialism*, of which there are many, form the majority opinion nowadays; the philosopher Daniel Dennett calls materialism an "opinion approaching unanimity," which is an overstatement. His carefully reasoned book *Consciousness Explained*[2] has been widely quoted and praised as providing definitive answers to the most puzzling aspects of the mind-body problem. It is easy to refute the existence of a mind that is independent of a brain, and the idea that bodily actions could be influenced by a nonphysical *entity* contradicts everything we know about nature. If the body is the deterministic machine Descartes claimed it is, then only physical forces should be able to affect its actions.

Does it follow then that man is "just a machine"? This is the inevitable conclusion in what I will call *orthodox materialism*. The machine cited most often for this metaphor is the modern digital computer, which—given appropriate *software* (elaborate instructions entered into the machine memory)—can imitate any real machine or process, however complex. The brain in Dennett's phrase is such a *virtual machine*.

Still, there are thoughtful dissenting voices: *The Emperor's New Mind*, by the English physicist Roger Penrose;[3] *Bright Air, Brilliant Fire*, by the American biologist and Nobel laureate Gerald Edelman;[4] and *Consciousness Revisited*[5] and *The Rediscovery of Mind*,[6] by the American philosophers Owen J. Flanagan and John R. Searle, respectively. Why are we so reluctant to accept the materialist interpretation of mind? It is partly because such *mental* qualities as feelings and consciousness remain unexplained, and partly because we suspect that a purely physical theory of brain function carries with it the grim implications of a clocklike determinism and predictability, or at least the absence of anything like free will. It also follows that the machinery of our brain, although intricate, can in principle be duplicated, and with it all the properties we associate with mind, including consciousness, the sensation of selfhood, imagination, and creativity. Eventually, the machine may excel in all these faculties and replace humans as the dominant species.

In the theory I will present here, I will shun the computer metaphor (which is flawed), and replace materialism (an outdated concept left over from nineteenth-century physics) with a more up-to-date *physicalism*. By this I mean the working assumption that physical processes ultimately must account for mental phenomena. For this the arsenal of contemporary physics already offers a richness of possibilities undreamed of only a few decades ago. I will propose specific mechanisms that are conceptually simple yet open the door to the unpredictable, to the flow of thought and the vagaries of creativity.

༺༺༺༺

The mind-body problem is not the only dualist dilemma we face. Chasms separate the individual from the rest of the cosmos, life from the inanimate, humans from animals, man from machine, image from reality. We make the distinctions between members of each pair by painstaking definitions, only to seek unity again by building elaborate bridges across the chasms. We consider unification to be an intellectual triumph. We succeed only rarely, and every one of these dualisms is an open question in our attempt to define ourselves.

In Judeo-Christian culture, humans, until the mid-nineteenth century, viewed themselves as unique creatures, the only ones in creation made in God's image, the only ones endowed with souls. They were able to overlook the startling resemblance they bore to the rest of the animal kingdom. Man was man and beast was beast. Denying animals a soul was an expression of man's feeling that his position in the universe was both singular and solitary.

Darwin's theory of evolution changed all that. Although animals had been worshiped in antiquity, it was only after the realization of evolutionary kinship that we thought much about animal pain and emotions. Except for the rearguard action of a few creationists, we now see man firmly embedded in, and related to, all other terrestrial life.

What makes the theory of evolution so remarkable is the enormous simplification and unification it imposes on the panorama of life on earth. But a gap remains. We are not just another species. Our ability to reason, our ingenuity, and our linguistic skills place us so far above any competing animal species that many of us feel that something beyond the mechanisms of evolution must have occurred to produce *homo sapiens*. Or perhaps a unique mutation freed our brains from the constraints of instinct and gave us a *mind*. The sociobiologist Edward O. Wilson dubbed it the *Promethean gene*.[7]

What distinguishes us more than anything else, however, is our acute awareness of a *self*, and a mental preoccupation with our own being that goes far beyond the kind of self-preserving behavior that all animals exhibit. Our strong sensation of selfhood often gives rise to a feeling of ineffable solitude, an existential angst engendered by an *outside world*, the *it* that surrounds the lone *I*.

But what is the nature of the *I*, of this subjective existence? How does it come about? By what mechanisms does it arise in our brains?

Bordering the outside world are our own bodies. We call them *ours*, but they are also part of the physical world, the world of objects. We know our bodies through the senses of pain and pleasure; we are concerned about them and depend on their well-being. We could not exist without them. But if *they* are part of the world around us, who are *we*, around whom this world is displayed?

We try to escape in different ways from this painful dualism, this stark cosmic solitude. The pious find solace in the belief in eternally caring deities and in a universe designed specifically to become the home for human beings. The latter is also the assertion of the *anthropic principle*, a theory that has come out of physics and astronomy. It holds that the evolving universe, long before life appeared on earth, was a benign system from the start, its laws and the so-called constants of nature delicately balanced to make possible the emergence of life and to facilitate the evolution of man.

This almost theistic conception of a benign universe that had man in mind almost from its violent start is to be contrasted with a world that often appears brutal and uncaring. We may destroy ourselves in a nuclear holocaust, Camille Paglia points out, but ''nature will absorb it all. After the bomb, nature will pick up the cards, shuffle them, and begin the game again. Nature is forever playing solitaire with herself.''[8]

Nature as friend, or nature the implacable? We court nature in many ways. In natural science we seek a bond with the cosmos through knowledge. We try to strip away some of the strangeness in nature by listening carefully to her pulse, and we gain some measure of oneness through understanding. It seems to be a never-ending process. Mysticism and magic try to achieve the same thing in a different way. The mystic lays claim to a hidden, private connectedness with the universe. But the question "Where do we fit in?" persists.

❧❧❧❧

Accident or providence, at some time during the physical evolution of the planet earth, life appeared as though a seed had been dropped into a sterile but fertile ground. This is indeed one of the many theories of the origin of life on earth.[9] Most scientists, however, favor the opinion that this *animation* of earth happened gradually and spontaneously, starting with very primitive prebiotic forms.

In the course of long geologic epochs amid a profusion of species, a creature evolved that was to become very different from the rest of the animal kingdom. *Homo sapiens* left his evolutionary niche some hundred thousand years ago and embarked on a course on which imagination and creativity became more valuable than swiftness and strength. Our biological similarity notwithstanding, the difference between humans and our nearest evolutionary cousins is profound. No animal ever carved the face of a human into a cave wall or gained control over fire.

Our environment has undergone the most profound changes, mostly due to our own intervention, but we remain biologically unchanged. We have every reason to believe that, if one of our forebears from the paleolithic past were brought to life, he or she would have no difficulty competing in all the skills that our technological society requires. We ascribe this adaptability, this seeming independence from biological constraints, to a unique possession, evolution's last gift to man: his *mind*.

But in what form do we possess this gift? Calling it the *Promethean gene*, as Wilson did, suggests that it is a physical, inherited characteristic, most likely residing in the brain. We therefore must examine this organ of mind.

A formidable array of disciplines, the *neurosciences*, has evolved, mostly in the last few decades, with the aim of understanding brain structure and function. The questions most frequently asked—and in some instances answered—are "How does neural circuitry distinguish between different inputs?" and "How is that information used to produce different reactions?" The brain is viewed and studied as an input-output device, appropriately called the *sensorimotor brain*. Can we explain all of the manifestations of mind in this manner? Is mind a function of the brain, as digestion is a function of the stomach, or is it an excretion of the brain, as bile is an excretion of the liver?

We will seek the mind-producing powers of the brain by examining how our senses generate neural messages about the world, and how these messages are transformed on their way to higher brain centers.

In vision, man's dominant sense, *images* are picked up at the retina of each eye and transported along the visual pathway to a succession of brain centers, where they are transformed, sifted, and mixed with other information. We shall see how the pattern of neural activity starts out as a replica of the pattern of light projected onto the retina. But after a few transformations, it bears no more resemblance to the original scene, and probably could not be interpreted by anyone even if it were known in its entirety. This raises the question of how the brain is able to refer these garbled messages back to the reality outside.

How, in other words, do *I* sense, perceive, and interpret this neural cryptogram in my head? If I could observe it the way an operator of a complex machine or system observes an instrument panel of gauges and indicator lights, it would be as meaningless to me as it would be to any other observer. And yet the information becomes transformed in my head from the seemingly chaotic firing patterns involving millions of neurons into something we can talk about again: perception, recognition of familiar forms, associations, emotions. As we proceed along the sensory pathways toward higher brain centers, it becomes more meaningful to talk not about neural firing patterns but about images and thoughts. We switch from brain talk to mind talk.

This raises a dual question: How are the mental images related to the corresponding objects and events in the outside world, and how are these mental functions related to strictly physical processes in the brain? What does my thought or mental image of a giraffe have to do with a real giraffe, and what is the physical state of the brain when I think of a giraffe?

In answer to the first question we can say that mental images are not just replicas of corresponding objects in the real world. They are compounded by meanings and associations derived from a lifetime of experiences. The image does not behave, therefore, like the corresponding physical reality, and its dynamics are not constrained by the laws that govern the behavior of physical objects.

But the fact that the image of a stone does not always behave like a stone—we can make it *fall* upward if we want to—does not exclude the possibility that thoughts have a solid physical basis. If the image is not simply a mental replica of reality, can we at least identify it with another physical reality, namely, the physical state of the brain itself? It has been argued, in another grand attempt at unification, that there is a strict relationship between our thoughts and the activity of the neurons in the brain. A thought, it is argued in this *psychoneural identity theory*, is just another way of talking about a particular sequence of physical events in the brain. A mental state *is* a brain state. On this assumption, the recall of a particular event in memory also could be described as the simultaneous activity of a specified, or at least specifiable, set of neurons.

This kind of description should please the physicist. In classical physics, physical states lend themselves to precise specification and hold out hope of valid predictions once the dynamics of the system are understood. The computational task may be daunting, but, in principle, it is argued, we should be able to predict the progression of our thoughts, just as we are able to predict the trajectory of a spacecraft tumbling through a complicated gravitational field.

This is the view I call *orthodox materialism*. It is based on classical—that is, nineteenth-century—physics, which, even today, is wrongly considered by some philosophers to be *the* scientific approach. Modern physics, which began in the early part of this century with the revolutionary concepts of relativity and quantum mechanics, has fundamentally altered the physicist's outlook. The machine that runs with deterministic precision like a perfect clock is no longer an adequate description for most processes in nature. There is no reason why it should apply to the brain. Paul Davies, a noted Australian physicist and writer, put it succinctly: "Materialism is dead."[10]

This does not mean that we should not look for mechanisms operating in the vast network of neurons for clues and explanations of mental phenomena. We will do just that, and we will talk at length about one mechanism that my students and I have written about extensively. We called it the *creative loop*.

A central problem in trying to devise a physical model of the mind has to do with the question of unification of our cognitive functions. It has been felt that—because a single self appears to be doing all the seeing, hearing, and thinking—there must be a place in the brain where everything comes together.

But first everything is scattered. Our sensory systems collect messages about the outside world in the form of images or neural codes. Hierarchies of neural analyzers are tuned to pick up the presence of specific features. In the visual system alone we find a special brain center concerned with color discrimination, another with motion, and apparently many shape-specific centers. Some neurons, or neuron groups, signal the presence of a single line segment of a particular orientation and location in the field of vision. Others appear to be tuned to patterns as complex as a human face.

The information picked up by the eye as a complete replica of the physical scene outside is dispersed among many different centers by the time it reaches the highest neural levels, the *cerebral cortex*.

Although I have the distinct impression that a single *I* views and is aware of all these features, there appears to be no place in the brain where it is all reassembled into a complete image. This dilemma has given rise to the myth of an immaterial presence, a spooky homunculus, who observes the state of the physical brain. The many feature-specific analyzers are then regarded as an instrument panel with flashing lights, gauges, and other indicators from which an intelligent operator draws valid conclusions. Another metaphor philosophers use is that of a theater, a stage, populated by many actors presenting many scripts, all of it unified through the eyes of the observer. For Descartes the pineal gland was such a stage.

But if there is a stage, the single observer of it all is missing. There now is a strong consensus that the putative *unification* of sensory perceptions and their elaborations into associations, thoughts, and so on, is nothing but a figment of our imagination. The notion has become popular among philosophers and neuroscientists that the human mind consists of a multiplicity of *processors*; Dennett speaks of "armies of idiots," each working on its own *draft* of reality.

This notion, the result of a laudable desire to avoid a metaphysical *I* that looks down from above, also deprives us of the means to give a physical account of our feelings of selfhood and apparent cognitive unity.

I will argue in the course of much of this book that we can have unification without homunculi. We have erroneously looked for the stage and its observer at the highest levels of cerebral processing. Instead, I will make a case for an inversion of sensory processing through which images are re-created and projected on screens near the bottom of the sensory pathways where they originated in the first place. Here sensory input and cortical fancy interact and often compete. The observer of the drama played out there is none other than the brain itself, which analyzes and re-creates, and then observes its own creations. This self-referent process is the *creative loop*.

We shall see that—unlike other physical theories of brain functions—this process breaks the vise of determinism and admits the unpredictable. I will make a case that those functions that we identify most strongly with human mind—imitation and invention— can be understood as manifestations of this process.

I single out imitation and invention because I believe that they are the basis of all creative activity. To cross the gap from the known to the unknown, from the familiar to the new, the mind first imitates what is known. We must presume that before making a stone tool, man *imitated* the natural fracturing of stone and the resulting sharp edge. He then *invented* the tool.

With our inventions we have endowed inanimate matter with properties previously possessed only by living things: *purpose* and *function*. The tool, and later the machine, are the products of *creative animations* of matter, by which I want to express that they did not evolve spontaneously, like life, but bear a resemblance to life because they can function and malfunction.

The analogy becomes more profound as the intricacy of our machines increases. Throughout, we see imitation as the forerunner of invention, until, in what many consider the ultimate triumph of our ingenuity, we imitate life and human intelligence. These attempts not only call for the most advanced of our technology but also challenge our conception of who and what we are.

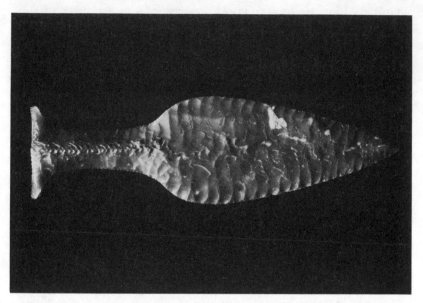

The Hindsgavl flint dagger, circa 1800–1500 B.C. (by permission of Nationalmuseet, Kopenhagen).

The mimicking of human life is a process driven as much by the exercise of cleverness as by a desire to understand our own nature. By pressing technology to the utmost to make the best imitation of human faculties, we become aware of that portion of humanness that is still beyond our comprehension and technological reach.

The evolution of technology thus sharpens the old mind-body dilemma. Can we endow a machine with a mind? How do we know when we have succeeded? Are we perhaps a vanishing species that will be replaced sooner or later by the clearer, faster, more reliable syllogisms of future supercomputers? In a world teeming with our likenesses, translated into electronic wizardry, some see our role as that of idle bystanders, drones to be exterminated eventually by a race of ambitious robots, unless we die first of sheer boredom. Such a scenario—the *death of man* or, if you will, the merging of the *I* with the *it*—is envisioned frequently in postmodernist writings.

Some writers have expressed the hope that human mind still can be saved. O. B. Hardison, in his visionary and thought-provoking *Disappearing Through the Skylight*,[11] suggests that mind could be attached to a silicon body and brain instead of being "fastened to a dying animal," in the words of William Butler Yeats.

It could then be lofted from its terrestrial vault into limitless space and endless time.

But I will be cautiously pessimistic. The time is not yet ripe for us to pin our hopes on silicon immortality. The fate of every *I* is to die with the animal. Perhaps it will always be this way.

Nor are our machines acquiring minds of their own. Our rush to attribute independent intelligence and personality to them is only the reflection of our deep-seated yearning to find and define ourselves, in the same sense that Thomas Mann once called man "the result of God's curiosity about Himself." Our inventions are still doing our bidding and will remain complementary to, rather than competitive with, our needs and faculties. This is why we have created them.

PART ONE

THE UNIVERSE

> *We think why*
> *because we think*
> *because.*
> *Because we think*
> *we think*
> *the universe is about us.*
> *But does it think*
> *the universe?*
> *Then what about?*
> *About us?*

From *The Universe*, May Swenson

Chapter 1

The *I* and the *It*

The division between the physical and the mental was formalized some three hundred years ago by the French philosopher René Descartes, and has since become known as the *Cartesian cut*. It makes a sharp distinction not only between the bodily and mental self but between the *I* and the *it*, that is, between the sensing, feeling, and thinking human and the sensed, felt, and thought-about world at large, a small but significant part of which is my own body.

❀❀❀❀

Let us begin with a perspective on these two protagonists in our story: the *I* and the *it*. The cut between the two has not always existed. In the medieval *City of God*, man was a central and privileged creature. The rest of the universe—the beasts and the inanimate world—were background, but part of the scheme of things. Not only was man the centerpiece of creation, his home, the earth, occupied the very center of the universe. His outlook was deeply religious. Medieval cosmology supported the ecclesiastic notion of a man-centered universe. According to ideas going back to Aristotle, the moon, the sun, the planets, and all the stars moved in perfect circles, as in a celestial dance, around our earth.

About a hundred years before Descartes, the Polish astronomer Nicolaus Copernicus proposed a revolutionary idea in his book *De revolutionibus orbium coelestium*: the earth was not the immobile center of the universe, but one of the planets orbiting a central sun. It was not long before the Catholic Church realized the gravity of this concept, which removed man from the center of creation and took away his faith in his own central role in the cosmos.

For a while, scientists were to pay dearly for espousing Copernican ideas. Galileo was forced by the Inquisition, under threat

3

of torture, to renounce his belief in a central sun. But by Newton's time, toward the end of the seventeenth century, the Copernican world order was firmly established. Nature, no longer ancillary to human existence, became more awesome but also more interesting. The world was now an *object* to be scrutinized dispassionately.

The fact that the earth was moving swiftly through space inspired the study of motion and of the forces that affect motion. Are angels pushing the earth along its path through space? Why aren't we sliding off the speeding globe? Why aren't birds left behind the moment they take to the air?

With every satisfactory answer gleaned, we gathered more confidence in the analytical power of our mind. With it also grew our appetite for more knowledge and more understanding. The pursuit of the natural sciences was under way. More and more, man's position was overshadowed by the unfolding grandeur of the universe. By comparison, his appearance seemed incidental and without significance. Nineteenth-century science had us stumble into this world as if by accident, virtual strangers even on our own outback planet, and destined to be obliterated by a mere shrug of its capricious nature. While success in the natural sciences was rapid and spectacular, the study of man was at first plodding and controversial and finally ended in the pronouncement that man is a machine.[1]

With the role of the *I* thus diminished, the *it*—the physical world, or *world of objects*, as I will call it—became progressively transformed, with its three distance scales moving ever farther apart. The scale of the middle distances, of everyday life, in which objects are neither very much larger nor very much smaller than our own bodies, has shrunk around us, threatening to suffocate us with the objects and images created by our technology and with our detritus. Today we are sick of being surrounded by the amplified real or simulated human images and voices that have crowded out everything nonhuman in the world of middle distance. What we yearn for is the nonhuman, the primeval: nature.

Meanwhile, the world of large distances, the cosmos, full of bizarre objects, has expanded to unimaginable vastness. At the other end of the scale, the world of the very small, first entered by us in the seventeenth century with the invention of the microscope, has opened up into a microcosm in which smallness transcends anything that still could be called matter. The universe had become a deluge of diversity.

❀❀❀❀

An examination of *my* side of the Cartesian gap reveals a microcosm that is different in every way. Where the world of objects is a world of dissembled diversity, my *self* suggests a monolithic oneness. The pathological *multiple personality* is almost an oxymoron. Its unitary character admits no scale. While the body defines the scale of *middle distances*—to be distinguished from the microscopic on one side and the cosmological scale on the other—the mind is neither large nor small. Space loses its metric character, and time, as we shall see, is ill defined.

The rules that seem to hold on my side of the Cartesian cut are different from the ones that govern the world of objects. I have been immersed all my life in a world of gravity, but in my dreams I can soar. I have been surrounded by a world that appears convincingly deterministic, leaving no room to doubt that strict rules of causality are behind everything observed. Yet, my mind still finds it odd that, try as I may, I cannot predict or influence the tumble of dice or the bouncing of the ball on a roulette wheel, and—as familiar as I am with the laws of probability—I am likely to succumb to the lure of a premonition in choosing numbers in a lottery.

I find it hard to accept that a fact as evident now as the ball on the roulette wheel having dropped into the slot numbered *fourteen* could not have been anticipated a second before the croupier closed the betting with his monotone "les jeux sont faites." We prefer to give credence to stories about people who dream of sequences of numbers and then walk away with a fortune the next day. It seems that our intuition is still wrestling with the arrow of time and the irreversibility of most physical events.

There is, I believe, an explanation for this. Past, present, and future are interwoven in my mind, and often interchangeable, in sharp contrast to events in the world of objects. The familiar *déjà vu* phenomenon is the most striking but by no means the only example of this scrambling of time and space in the world of the mind. Vladimir Nabokov, in *King, Queen, Knave*, speaks of the "no-time of human thought," and in T. S. Eliot's words, "to be conscious is not to be in time." We will come back to this in later chapters and seek a neurological basis for this phenomenon.

My mind often strains against what I perceive to be the *laws of nature*, and would prefer to live in a world of magic. Many of us succumb to the lure of the occult. Francis Bacon, the Renaissance philosopher who was among the first to define a scientific approach, called the mind "an enchanted glass, full of superstition and imposture,"[2] and Albert Einstein, some three hundred years later, acknowledged that every scientist is a "tamed metaphysicist."[3]

The world of objects is not really my world. I have no possessions there that are truly my own. I am like a stranger at a rich man's gate. What I have is borrowed, and even my knowledge is nothing but hand-me-downs, and an occasional oddity I pick up by chance. I pass it on to others like me.

The world of objects is a world of permanence that contrasts startlingly with my own passing presence. This is not just a matter of degree. You may object that even stars that last billions of years have a preordained lifetime. They are born and they die.

Not so. That is a mortal's viewpoint. Behind all changes, even cataclysmic changes, stands the immutable constancy of such fundamental descriptors of nature as energy, momentum, and a host of other *invariants*. It has been said that the physicist's way of understanding any process in nature is to demonstrate that, in fact, no fundamental change has taken place. Stars are not born, nor do they die. They are merely one of the ever-changing forms that matter or energy takes on, from diffuse clouds of dust and gas swirling through space to the hydrogen- and helium-burning suns, and finally—no, never *finally*—to the supernovas that collapse into the nothingness of black holes while exploding at the same time into the stuff from which they were made originally: more swirling clouds of dust and gas expanding into space. But now new types of atoms have been formed, carbon, nitrogen, oxygen, and all the heavier atomic species without which life could not have come into existence. As for the black holes: they are suspected by some physicists to be the *cosmic eggs* from which new universes are born.

We try to set limits of time and space to the world of objects, so that we can encompass them with our mind. It is easier to comprehend a universe that started with a *big bang* and will end in a *big crunch* than one that has no beginning and no end. Some current cosmological theories postulate the existence of other universes that may spring up like mushrooms from black holes or from "seeds" that are unimaginably small fluctuations in the physicist's vacuum. We understand the words but cannot fathom their implications.

The person I call my *self* is unlike most objects around me that are composed of particular bits of matter. It is not the atoms in my body that constitute my *self*. They take only temporary abode here. Few of them stay with me for very long, and new ones soon take their places. If I were to tag the atoms and molecules in my brain, heart, lungs, and so on, I would find that I have very little in common with the person I was only a few years ago. That would seem to make me a diffuse, ill-defined entity. On the contrary, in all the material structures of this universe, there is no boundary anywhere as sharp, as absolute, as that delimiting the individual from the rest of the world.

My identity problem has something in common with that of a waterfall. The water going over it this second will be many miles downriver tomorrow, and new floods will preserve its apparent reality. This is not a new problem. Heraclitus wrestled with it more than twenty-five hundred years ago when he marveled that everything is in flux.

But I question that there really is such a thing in the cosmos as a waterfall. Let me explain. The world of objects is a *dissembled world*, where each bit of matter follows its own course, isolated from all the others in space and time. Each water droplet falls by itself, independent of the millions of other droplets falling along with it. It knows nothing about the others, nor about the rushing stream above or the thundering pool below. The same goes for the atoms in each droplet of water, and when we descend to the quarks and fields that are the essence of the atoms, we are in a world that certainly knows no waterfalls. Indeed, *knowing* has no meaning anywhere in the world of objects.

You might object that the laws of physics bind together all material objects, drawing on their past and determining their future. The earth, to take another example, is bound to orbit the sun, which, through its gravitational attraction, guides each planet along well-defined *trajectories* that stretch from remote past to distant future, and on which the present is a sliding point separating the two.

But trajectories are only a physicist's subjective scheme of organizing reality. Also, the sun does not reach out and tug on the earth. In reality, the earth, and every part of it, merely senses the gravitational field in which it finds itself, and knows nothing about a sun ninety-three million miles away, any more than the sun knows of its family of planets, comets, and asteroids. This follows from what in contemporary physics is called *local causality,* which, in turn, arises from *local interaction.*

We now think of forces as caused by *fields.* This amounts to the statement that any action between objects is propagated from point to neighboring point in space and cannot travel faster than light. An event taking place *here* at this *moment* cannot have an effect somewhere else at the same time. It cannot leap, but must pull itself along in space like a wave on a taut rope. This is the meaning of *local interaction* and *local causality.*

We have already mentioned the absence of scale in the world of the mind. Local causality is meaningless here; unlike the dissembled world of objects, the world of images that constitutes my mind is an *assembled* world in which all events coexist as a tightly cross-linked network, and past, present, and future are knit together in a single fabric, distinguishable like threads of different colors, but tightly interwoven.

Let us return to the world of objects again to get a firmer grasp of the essential difference in the character of the two realms.

When Isaac Newton discovered that a universal law of gravitation was the key to the motions of planets and moons, the sun was pictured as pulling on every bit of matter in our solar system in a manner termed *action-at-a-distance.* Quite unlike any force previously encountered, this force seemingly required no intervening material connection, no strings, no cables. It was believed then that it could be felt instantly across millions of miles of empty space. This seemed puzzling but was accepted as fact.

Modern physicists reject the notion of an action-at-a-distance and recognize only local interactions. In this new picture, the sun does not *reach out* across space and pull on each planet. Instead, the sun, being a very large body, *warps* the space that surrounds it, creating a domain of eminence around itself, a *field.* The earth and the other planets, finding themselves in this warped space, are constrained to follow the dictates of local interaction, much like steel ball bearings rolling over a warped sheet of metal. Every particle of matter merely senses (that, too, is anthropomorphic) the conditions at its own location, the curvature of space, and behaves accordingly, each one a universe to itself, so to speak. Space, to any object, is its own space, wherever it happens to be. Time is always the present. There is no other.

The world of objects may be said to lack both past and future. Only the present exists, but it is an existence of total isolation in space and time for every speck of dust, for every atom in the universe. The conditions of this moment cease to exist a moment later, and no future event exists before it becomes the present. No influence is exerted across finite time gaps, just as, in space, there is no action-at-a-distance. Present events result from present conditions, that is, conditions that are *contiguous* in space and time. The past has dropped out of existence. It is only the equations of physics, or our less rigid memories and intuitions, that allow us to extrapolate over an infinity of such infinitesimal contiguities and to make statements about past or future events.

Einstein, who was a firm believer in local causality, expressed this by saying that it is "an essential aspect of this arrangement of things in physics that they lay claim, at a certain time, to an existence independent of one another, provided these objects are situated in different parts of space."[4]

The principle of local causality has not remained without challenge, but most contemporary physicists still regard it as one of the touchstones of their science.

In the world of objects, then, everything is discrete, but with me nothing exists in isolation. When I meet a friend in the street, our years of past friendship are conjured up the instant I recognize him, and I know that in the next moment I will stop, shake hands with him, and exchange a few words. Objects are replaced by images. But the images are not the kind we see rolling off a movie film or videotape, which show well-defined *sequences* of events.

The human mind is the *joiner*, fitting together the disparate elements of the world to make objects, systems, sceneries. It can bridge distances from the size of an atom's nucleus to the space between galaxies, and leap over time spans of millennia as nimbly as over seconds. Contemplating the myriad isolated existences in the world of objects, my mind fits them all together into a universe. I remember or reconstruct what no longer exists and call it the *past*. I project or guess at what has not yet happened and call it the *future*. I connect the past with the present and invent purpose, a kind of nonlocal causality. I do the same with present and future, and create *intentionality*, also hope and fear. All of these are constructs of the mind, because neither past nor future exists in the world of objects.

It is *I* who makes the waterfall. I gather up a hundred billion suns and make a galaxy. I link galaxies across vast spaces and plot their past and future to the beginning and the end of time, and then wonder at the meaning of these limits. I perceive the juxta-position of myriad atoms in a pebble and create its roundness, its color, texture, its *gestalt*. In the language of quantum mechanics, I observe and measure, and cause the system I observe to fall into a definite state.

❁❁❁❁

What is it about the stuff that temporarily makes up my body, my brain, that places it outside the world of objects and yet gives it the power to draw together objects that are worlds apart? What strange faculty allows me to provide unity and connectedness to objects, where otherwise there would be only timelessness and isolation? How do thoughts, feelings, and our sense of selfhood arise from the machinery in our heads? How does the brain make a mind? And how does the joiner mind link us to the rest of the universe?

Chapter 2

What *It* Has Done for *Us*

The natural sciences of the eighteenth and nineteenth centuries have, as we have seen, diminished man's supposed role and pictured the natural world as indifferent to human needs.

This is not to say that nature has not provided us with just the right amount of everything that makes our lives possible. Therein lies the big quandary. The sun is just the right distance from the earth to keep us warm without scorching. The earth and its atmosphere have all the right ingredients in just the right proportions to supply us with food and shelter. We would call nature *benevolent*, were it not for the generally accepted scientific dogma that there is no planning, no purpose, no *providence* in nature. It does not *provide*. It happens to have what we happen to need. Is it all just one string of fortuitous, but incredibly unlikely, accidents?

This view was expressed most forcefully by the French biologist and Nobel laureate Jacques-Lucien Monod in his book *Chance and Necessity*. "The universe," he stated, "was not pregnant with life nor the biosphere with man. Our number came up in a Monte Carlo game."

One result of this downgrading of the role of humans has been a deepening chasm between science and the humanities, for which C. P. Snow coined the expression the *two cultures*. It has led to a distrust of science on the part of people more interested in human problems and human aspirations. Lately, there have been many attempts to reconcile the two outlooks, that is, to create a scientific view that moves man back toward the hub of things. The evolutionary theorist Erich Jantsch speaks of bringing together science and the humanities in a unified view."[1]

11

The Anthropic Principle

Perhaps the boldest attempt to reunite what Copernicus had severed four and a half centuries earlier, and to explain away the incredible accident of our existence, goes by the name of the *anthropic principle.*

The character of the universe is determined by the *laws of nature* and by some numbers that appear arbitrary, that is, not derivable from any law. One of these is the exact ratio of the masses of the two constituents of atomic nuclei: the proton and the neutron. If this number were only slightly different, the world would be so drastically different that what we know as life could not exist. And, if the electric charge on the electron or the strength of the gravitational force were changed by minute amounts, there would be no atoms, no stars or planets—again a universe totally hostile to anything resembling life.

One of the most startling *accidents* is the existence of carbon in the universe. We are carbon-based creatures. The chemistry of our bodies is carbon chemistry. No carbon—no life. But there was no carbon in the beginning of the universe. The only elements created in the first few minutes following the big bang were hydrogen, helium, and traces of lithium, the three lightest. After that, element formation ceased. When the first stars and galaxies were formed much later, their initial composition was the same as that of the primordial stuff: 75 percent hydrogen, 25 percent helium, traces of lithium. Nothing else. Certainly no carbon.

The formation of heavier elements began deep in the cores of the first stars in processes we call thermonuclear reactions. Physicists have found, however, that there appeared a formidable barrier. To form a nucleus of carbon 12, the lighter nuclei of beryllium 8 and helium 4 would have to collide and fuse. But beryllium 8 is so short-lived (it can exist for only about 0.000000000000001 of a second) that the process could not have happened with sufficient frequency.

There was one remote possibility. If it so happened that the carbon nucleus had a high energy state, what physicists call an *excited* state, at just the right level, there would be a *resonance* to the carbon-producing reaction, very much like the tuned string of a musical instrument that resonates to sound of the right frequency. Such an excited state in carbon was looked for—and found exactly at the energy where it was needed. We owe our lives to that fortuitous energy state in the carbon atom.

Why, then, are these numbers just right to allow us to be here and ask these questions? John D. Barrow and Frank Tipler, one a contemporary astrophysicist, the other a specialist in general relativity and gravitation, give this answer: "It is not only that man is adapted to the universe. The universe is adapted to man." John Wheeler, also a noted relativist, goes further, saying that "a life-giving factor lies at the center of the whole machinery and design of the world."[2] But if the world machine was thus "pregnant with life," to use Monod's expression, then we would be able to assign function and purpose to events all the way back to the big bang: the purpose was the future evolution of life and the eventual appearance of man; function was any process that enhanced that goal. The origin of life, the *animation* of the universe, would seem less of an abrupt change since it was already implicit in the workings of the inanimate world.

Barrow and Tipler, in *The Anthropic Cosmological Principle*, define at least three anthropic principles: WAP, SAP, and FAP. The *weak* anthropic principle (WAP) doesn't say much: Here we are, and the world is what it is. If it were any different, we wouldn't be here. The *strong* version (SAP) is more like Wheeler's statement above. It asserts that there is *purpose* in the design of the universe, built into it from its very beginning, and the purpose is *man*. The *final* anthropic principle (FAP) is the most sweeping: "Intelligent information processing must come into existence in the universe, and, once it comes into existence, it will never die out." Barrow and Tipler are quick to point out that only WAP can be taken for granted. SAP and FAP are pure speculation.

The two stronger of the anthropic principles imply not only purposiveness but also what is often called *top-down* control. It means that primitive features of a system are controlled by complex processes operating on a higher level. The invention of a deity is one way of explaining top-down control. Other than that, top-down control seems to be limited to living systems. (The microstructure of the DNA molecule is determined by the interaction of a species with its environment.) Thus the numbers that determine the energy levels in carbon, or the proton-neutron mass ratio, are regulated by such high-level phenomena as the appearance of life and intelligence.

The strong anthropic principle not only requires turning causality upside down—having top-down, instead of the ordinary bottom-up, control—but, somehow, causality has to also work backward in time. The requirements of life must have exerted their influence on events preceding its first appearance by billions of years. Barring such strange time reversal, somebody or something must have peered into the future and concluded that for life to evolve, carbon had to be formed in stars, and it was therefore necessary to endow carbon with that particular energy level. Then, even though the subsequent evolution of life was purely Darwinian, we must conclude that life was *created* by an intelligent being, that is, a being that had the power of foresight and purposive action. Such purposive action would imply a causality that is *nonlocal* in time, a leap into the future to formulate decisions in the present.

The above remarks pertain mostly to the two stronger versions of the anthropic principle; the weaker one avoids most of the strangeness but does not provide an alternative to the life-by-accident scenario. The choice between accident and providence is ultimately one of temperament and faith, which places it outside the boundaries of empirical science. My own feelings tend to agree with those of the late physicist Heinz Pagels, who wrote: "The influence of the anthropic principle on the development of contemporary cosmological models has been sterile. It has explained nothing. . . I would opt for rejecting the anthropic principle as needless clutter in the conceptual repertoire of science."[3] Monod expressed even more categorically what many contemporary scientists have taken as the orthodox scientific view:

> *[It is] our very human tendency to believe that behind everything real in the world stands a necessity rooted in the very beginning of things. Against this notion, this powerful feeling of destiny, we must be constantly on guard. Immanence is alien to modern science. Destiny is written concurrently with the event, not prior to it [Monod 1971].*

I believe, then, that function and purpose are concepts that have no meaning in the prebiotic world, and that the origin of life marked a fundamental change, although not necessarily an abrupt one, in the universe. We will talk next about this *spontaneous animation* from which we arose.

To accept the *great accident* hypothesis may not be as drastic a solution to the dilemma of life on earth. Since there was no function in the lifeless world, there was also no *malfunction*. One outcome would have been as good and as valid as another. Some four billion years ago the earth spun along its yearly trek around the sun, as it does now, creating night and day and—we can presume— seasons. But no creature was warmed by the sun or felt the chill of the night. No function was served by the changing of day into night and back to day again, no definable purpose to the progression of seasons. All these phenomena merely *happened* as a result of the inevitable interplay of untold numbers of particles and fields.

The laws of the physical universe and the choice of the baffling constants of nature were not decreed by a life-designing engineer. But life had to take the world as given and adapt to it as best it could. We see this tendency of life to fill every available niche with an appropriately adapted life form as a continuing process. New forms of bacteria have arisen that thrive and proliferate in tanks of jet fuel. It would be silly to say that we invented jet fuel to provide a habitat for new bacteria.

How unlikely was this crucial combination of circumstances that made life possible, how narrow our window of opportunity? What is the likelihood that the carbon atom have an energy level at just the right place?

I don't think we can answer this. Since we don't know how its existence is predicated on other facts, we don't know what other facts or constants would have to be changed to make that energy level disappear. Putting it another way, we can't just snip out an energy level from a universe of interdependent facts and ask "What if?" for the simple reason that such an intervention may be inconsistent with remaining facts. Hence, we have no idea what sort of a universe we would end up with, and whether in this hypothetical world anything self-organizing, evolving, and remotely lifelike could occur. We can say only that there would be nothing resembling us or any other beast on earth. Our inability to say more should be evident from the fact that, knowing what we do about this world, its laws and constants as they exist, we still would be unable to *predict* the origin of life (if we didn't know it), let alone calculate the course evolution has taken.

As to the improbability that the critical numbers such as the proton-neuron ratio, or the exact location of that energy level in carbon, have exactly the values needed by us, we were assuming that nature spun the wheels of chance, which happened to stop at all the right places. But the wheels may be constrained by laws still unknown to us, and what looks like chance may in fact be necessity.

Chapter 3

Spontaneous Animation

*We must, however, acknowl-
edge, as it seems to me that man with all his noble qualities. . .still bears in his bodily frame the indelible stamp
of his lowly orgin.*

Charles Darwin

With the appearance of life, *purpose* and *function* definitely had made their entrance in the physical universe. It is not the purpose of a stone to cling to the side of a cliff. If the force of gravity, the tug of the wind, or the hoof of a mountain goat overcomes the forces of adhesion in the rock, a piece of it will tumble down and join the thousands already in the scree below. I have often thought, when climbing in the Rocky Mountains, how easily one could convince oneself of the safety of a particular hold. It has been there, after all, for millions of years; surely it would not come off in the next second. Once I was given an object lesson in the fallacy of this argument, when a piece of the mountain the size of a small suitcase gave way under me. Luckily, the one above me held. It was not the rockface that failed. I did.

"The world doesn't happen," said the mathematician Hermann Weyl, "it simply *is*."

But something extraordinary did happen at the point when the first stirrings of life thrust themselves on this inanimate world, upsetting forever the edenic purposelessness of the prebiotic world.

The profound otherness of life has not always been realized. "The history of biology is the history of struggles over the difference between the animate and the inanimate," says the Harvard biologist Richard Lewontin, and then he points out that this history is a relatively brief one. It was not so long ago that the entire universe was seen as "a single interconnected system" in which "men

could be petrified and marble statues turned into warm flesh.''[1]
As late as the mid-nineteenth century it still was widely believed
that vermin could emerge spontaneously from dirt.

It was Louis Pasteur who first demonstrated convincingly that
life only came from life. We now know that every cell that is alive
today was simply formed from the living parts of other cells. There
is protoplasmic continuity going back to times immemorial, and
we have no reason to assume that a single cell ever formed out
of inanimate matter.

But life must have started somewhere, since the earth at the
time of its formation, and for more than a billion years after that,
almost certainly was sterile. Unless we believe in divine intervention or the introduction of life from outside the earth by accident
or design, we are faced with the problem of circumventing
Pasteur's dogma and contriving to build a bridge leading from the
inanimate to the living. Most biologists now believe that this *origin
of life* occurred spontaneously in an evolutionary process that led
from very complex chemistry, via largely unknown prebiotic forms,
to the purposive functioning of systems of matter we call organisms. This is what I call the *spontaneous animation* of matter.

Origin of Life

Biological evolution, as we understand it today, requires the
interaction of several processes. One is self-replication, the ability
of some complex structures to form copies of themselves. Another
is the occasional appearance of errors leading to heritable mistakes. With these two premises satisfied, the environment can exert its selective pressure to drive the progress of evolution. During
the later stages of evolution yet another process gains importance.
Sexual reproduction allows different types to be formed by combining pieces of genetic material from the two parents.

Only complex chemical systems are capable of carrying out
these functions. Where and how could such processes have
started?

Simple calculations convince one that random processes hardly
could have led to the necessary complexity. The British cosmologist
Fred Hoyle likens the chance of such random assemblies to that
of an intact 747 jumbo jet being assembled by a tornado sweeping
through a junkyard.

In 1953 Stanley L. Miller, then a young graduate student working in the laboratory of the well-known physical chemist Harold C. Urey at the University of Chicago, accomplished what appeared to be a giant step. In a sealed container he placed a mixture of substances—hydrogen, water vapor, ammonia, and methane—that were believed to have been representative of gases prevalent in the primitive atmosphere of the earth, some 3.5 billion years ago, before life appeared. Miller had placed no molecules of greater complexity into the enclosure, but after the mixture had been subjected to electrical discharges for several days, chemical analysis showed the presence of amino acids, the building blocks from which all proteins are made.

The discovery caused enormous excitement among biologists, but they soon realized that the path from Miller's simple amino acids to living cells was even more implausible than the creation of amino acids from the gases of the primitive earth. To link hundreds of amino acids together into a functional protein requires a blueprint we now attribute to ribonucleic acids (RNAs), another class of organic molecules, whose subunits—the ribonucleotides adenine, guanine, cytosine, and uracil—also are produced in Miller-type experiments. But the presence of RNA blueprints is not enough. The transcription of the RNA message and the linking of amino acids into protein chains require the presence of helpers, or *catalysts*, which are other proteins. The preservation and replication of the genetic information that specifies all proteins of a particular organism is now the function of yet another group of macromolecules, the deoxyribonucleic acids, or DNAs. True evolution in the biological sense cannot be simply selection, but must include a replicative feature. DNA provides the mechanism for self-copy, that is, *replication*. To start this cycle at any point requires the preexistence of very complex organic molecules.

The synthesis of large molecules cannot proceed without catalysts. In today's living world, the catalysts are proteins known as *enzymes*. Without catalysts the spontaneous formation of a molecule as complex as RNA would be so unlikely as to be practically ruled out. Such random chemistry can go as far as making amino acids, as in the Miller experiment, but not much farther. But the catalysts, or proteins, could not have been formed without RNAs existing first. It appeared to be an impasse.

It was discovered recently, however, that some RNAs can act as enzymes, promoting the construction of more RNAs from simpler constituents. Combining this property of self-replication with the Darwinian principle of selection would at last provide the powerful machinery of true biological evolution. All that was needed now was time.

This is a sketch of what the Harvard biologist Walter Gilbert has called the *RNA world*. The details of the chemical processes are far from being understood, and many difficulties remain. But assuming that these general ideas are correct, and some RNAs existed to start the process, the RNA world must have evolved for a long time, spawning a complex network of new adaptive forms. Eventually these were able to give rise to another group of biochemicals, the double-helix DNAs, then proteins, and eventually the first living cell.

Incorporated in that cell's delicate structure was a most precious evolutionary gift that had been accumulating through hundreds of millions of years of trials, replications, inherited mistakes, and more trials: the wisdom to maintain itself in a sea of adversity and to propagate its own kind. It is what Monod has called "the dream of every cell: to become two cells."

There is still the puzzle of how the RNA world came into existence in the first place. RNAs are complex enough that their formation by random chemistry is highly unlikely. Christian de Duve, who received the 1974 Nobel Prize in Physiology and Medicine, describes a plausible pathway leading from compounds that can be formed spontaneously, to the RNAs, by way of another network of *protoenzymes*, which he identifies as a group of sulfur-based organic molecules called *thioesters*.[2]

What emerges from all this is still far from a continuous account of the chain of events in the origin of life. Some biologists think we must look for extraterrestrial sources of the ingredients of life. But it appears at last that some plausible theories of a spontaneous, terrestrial origin of life have been advanced.

❀❀❀❀

With life established, the inevitable companion of function is its opposite: malfunction. The events that subserve the primary purpose of the mechanism occasionally fail to materialize, either because of inherent imperfections of the mechanism itself, because of occasional disturbances from the outside, or because of that everpresent byproduct of all physical processes: noise.

Thus, the delicate machinery of replication of the DNA molecule, the keeper of that most valuable blueprint of any life form, generally operates with almost flawless perfection. Every nucleotide of every gene is faithfully copied, and special molecular devices scan the new product for possible mistakes. Every living cell is witness to the precision of these molecular mechanisms. But some mistakes do occur, and a few of them remain uncorrected.

Most of us are fortunate to be free of such devastating genetic errors as hemophilia, sickle cell anemia, Huntington's disease, and others. But if such malfunctions threaten the individual whose well-being is the primary purpose of the replication mechanism, genetic *errors* are *functional* with respect to another, we may call it *higher*, purpose: Without such occasional misses, and the inevitable resultant harm to individuals of the species, there could be no evolution. Without such errors, which power the engine of all adaptive changes and the generation of new species, life on earth would never have advanced beyond the stage of the primitive precaryotic cell. In fact, it would have gotten stuck at a much more primitive stage.

It follows that, when we speak of function and purpose, we must have a particular process in mind. Also, it appears that the system whose purpose a particular process serves is generally of a more complex nature than the process itself. DNA replication serves the purpose of providing the blueprint for a normal living cell. The cell, in turn, functions to keep alive the organism to which it belongs. But replication errors (mutations) *function* in providing the necessary variability that allows the species to adapt to changing environments or to spawn new species.

I must emphasize that *purpose* here carries no connotation of foresight, of teleology. As in any good physical process, the outcome cannot occur before the cause. The function is not decreed by an agency or cosmic *mind* that knows the outcome of different scenarios and then puts into effect the circumstances that favor the selected outcome. Rather, purpose itself is both the result and the agent in that very natural phenomenon called evolution: If mutations are *functional*, serving to cause reproductive advantages, they accomplish this purpose without the ability to peek into the future. No process of reasoning, no computation that weighs and then selects among different available alternatives, is involved here. No *teleology*. But top-down control is exerted by the environment on the genetic material through the selective pressures exerted on the random mutations.

Most biologists, while readily discussing the function of this enzyme or that organ, are reluctant to talk of *purpose* in living systems, feeling that this would introduce metaphysical elements into their science. But here we run, it seems to me, into some logical difficulties. Can we really say that the functioning (normally pumping) heart has no purpose? Only its purpose—namely, the transport of oxygenated blood from the lungs to all body tissues and back to the lungs again—decides what is function and what is malfunction of the heart.

But again, purpose is to be viewed in the light of a particular process, generally of a higher order of complexity. A function such as random mutations of genes may, as we have seen, be detrimental in individual cases, but essential in adapting the species to changing environments. A particular protein may lose its function and become just extra baggage that evolution has not yet been able to shed. The same protein, having lost its original function, also may begin to serve a totally different function in the organism. This may be true also of entire organs. As an example of such *function change*, Konrad Lorenz cites the air bladder of fishes, used by them to control their buoyancy. When some species moved from sea to land, gills became superfluous and were discarded, but air bladders, no longer needed for swimming, evolved into the lungs of air-breathing terrestrial life.[3]

It would be wrong to say that air bladders of fishes were designed to become the lungs of land animals. But it also would be silly to deny the evident purpose of lungs, which is to oxygenate blood.

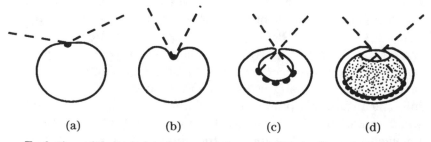

(a)   (b)   (c)   (d)

Evolution of the eye: (a) photosensitive spot; (b) pit; (c) pinhole camera; (d) eye with lens and retina.

The evolution of our eye illustrates how extremely delicate structures and intricate mechanisms can arise without teleology. Some unicellular organisms have developed light-sensitive spots, allowing them to orient themselves toward or away from a source of light. We may assume that the appearance of this primitive organ was the result of a series of random processes that were selected because they conferred an adaptive advantage to the cell. Later in evolution, a pit may have developed around the light-sensitive spot. This would have had the advantage of providing more directional discrimination. In multicellular organisms the pit deepened to become a cavity, and the partial closing of the entrance would have given the structure imaging properties similar to that of a pinhole camera. When the cavity filled with fluid it formed an optical lens, sharpening the image at the floor of the cavity, which became a retina. At no step was there planning. Recall again Monod's phrase that "destiny is written concurrently with the event, not prior to it."

I am not suggesting that the evolution of the eye proceeded in quite so simple and straightforward a fashion as depicted here. In species after species, new trial solutions and adaptations, and many abandoned strategies, appeared. But we can understand how a structure as delicate and apparently goal-directed as the eye could have arisen through the selection of many random events.

We conclude that the animation of matter that led to the appearance of life on earth was a *spontaneous* process, by which I mean one that arose in nature without preknowledge, without help from an agency endowed with the ability to look ahead by computation, simulation, or intuition and to affect the outcome by volitional acts.

❀❀❀❀

Where, in this long history of the animation of matter, are purpose and function, as we have defined them, first evident? With hindsight we might say that the emergence of the first amino acids in some primeval bolt of lightning presages life. So does the building up of heavier atoms in the nuclear cauldron of a star. But I would put the true beginnings of animation and the first interplay of purpose and function at the time of the first self-guiding catalytic chains of thioesters, if we accept de Duve's theory, and later of RNAs, processes that differ so profoundly from the random chemistry that went on before. There is no single instant in history when this occurred, but there must have appeared, gradually, a cleavage between the nascent life and an indifferent inanimate world.

Over the next few billion years, that gap has become deeper and wider. It is crossed only when an organism dies. Whether it can still be crossed in the opposite direction remains one of the burning questions in science.

Chapter 4

Creative Animation: End Before Cause

Go shroud your face in vapors, Zeus,
and, like a boy decapitating thistles,
practice on lofty oaks and mountain tops.
But you must leave my earth alone,
my cabin that you did not build,
my hearth, whose radiance you desire.

Goethe, *Prometheus*

If purpose and function are the hallmarks of animated matter, then the primitive handax that paleolithic humans fashioned from pieces of flint was animated matter also. It served to scrape hides, cut meat, and crush bone. It failed, when its cutting edge crumpled. But, unlike any of the life forms, it did not evolve, it was *created*.

I will therefore call this emergence of purpose and function among the objects of the physical world the *creative animation* of matter. The creators are almost exclusively humans, and the creations are called machines. They run the gamut from the most primitive Stone Age tools to the most sophisticated devices of our own age. We become awed by our creations when they begin to mimic properties previously possessed only by their creators: intelligence and the ability to plan ahead.

These features raise another dualism: that between life and its imitation by machines. But we must not forget the profound difference in the way the two came about. Look again at the evolutionary processes responsible for what we called the *spontaneous* animation of matter. There, processes were entirely accounted for by the strict rules of traditional physics. No peek into the future was allowed. If the history of evolution now appears to have led us toward a goal, this is entirely illusory. Evolution, biologists like

25

to point out, does not progress, it drifts. It does not seek better and better life forms, but merely adjusts to the ever-changing conditions in the environment. If in the process complexity tends to increase, this is due only to the fact that nature rarely starts out anew, but modifies, builds onto, existing organisms. Memory of past evolutionary events is frozen into the DNA of the species, and is therefore always part of the present. No future is envisioned. No enlightened guesses are made. No grand designer is at work. It is only through the eyes of an intelligent observer, looking backward, that evolutionary *trends* are perceived.

By contrast, our civilization evolves not by the agonizingly slow trial-and-error mutations in our genes, but by purposive and creative acts born in the human mind.

Toolmaking is the oldest creative activity, and still one of the most spectacular. To create a tool, even one as primitive as a paleolithic handax, requires more than serendipity, although accidents surely have played a role in many inventions. Concepts of need, of sharpness, of application, must have been in the mind of the creator before he started chipping at the rock. There was memory also of the type of stone that chipped best and held its edge. The end had to be envisioned before the creation could be caused. Intentionality must precede creativity. Richard Kearney calls it the *Hellenic imagination*, whose symbol, Prometheus, stands for "the power to anticipate the future by projecting an horizon of imaginary possibilities."[1]

True creative animation, I would argue, is almost solely the work of humans. Animals, too, use tools, but we must distinguish between an implement that comes ready made and one that requires deliberate fabrication. Picking up a stick for poking or beating, as some animals are capable of doing, may be considered as using tools, but it is not tool*making*, which must also be distinguished from such instinctive activities as building beehives, termite mounds, or birds' nests. Such structures may be quite elaborate, but they follow inherited behavior patterns that are most certainly the result of evolutionary adaptation. We would not say that birds are planning a family when they are building a nest. Compare such actions with a creative train of thought that may have gone through the mind of a paleolithic toolmaker:

> *I have noticed sharp edges where*
> *pieces of flint had chipped. I can visualize a stone of a certain*

size with one side chipped into a sharp edge, being used for scraping hides. I will therefore take a fist-sized rock and make one side into a cutting edge.

In the same way, the construction of every tool must have been preceded by mental activity in which an image, or concept, of the device was first envisioned in the mind of the creator. The imaginary object then was mentally tried, modified, and eventually constructed.

The stone ax was the beginning of a technology that culminated in today's supercomputers and superbombs. Man invented, created, and populated a previously indifferent inanimate world with machines that served his purposes. It is as though a spirit (*animus*) had been infused into objects to make them into animated matter.

In my student days, I drove an old automobile—the first one I ever owned—that used more oil than gasoline. One day it overheated badly, and by the time I reached a service station, steam was whistling from its radiator, and there was smoke and a stench of burnt oil coming from the bowels of the engine. The car was in acute distress. When the mechanic poured cool, clear lubricating oil into the crankcase, I could almost hear the engine respond with a sigh of relief.

Of course, the pistons really didn't care whether they moved smoothly up and down or ground themselves into the cylinder walls. There nevertheless was that vivid image of injury, almost of anguish, of a breakdown of synergism, of a loss of *esprit de corps* that normally links the moving parts of an automobile into a functioning, *animated* whole.

It is not difficult to see what was so animalistic about the ailing automobile. The machine was sick. Its normal state was disrupted by grossly malfunctioning parts. It is more difficult to understand what, if anything, set it apart from a sensing, suffering, living thing—but maybe not all that difficult.

To sense, to suffer, one must possess a central organ that supervises the actions of all parts of the organism and is aware of their harmonious or discordant response. There must be something equivalent to a brain. That is not to say that such a central organ guarantees suffering, but it is at least a prerequisite.

Well, my car certainly did not have a brain. It didn't even have a built-in computer, like cars have nowadays, since it was a product of the 1940s. And yet there *was* a brain that sensed and suffered, or at least showed concern about the well-being of that old car: *my* brain! It can be said to have performed for that automobile functions similar to those it performed, and still is performing, for me. It guided, controlled, and sensed many of the things that had to do with the functioning of the car, which thus was included in the extended domain of concern of my brain.

Being brain-guided, the automobile had its status raised from one of just *animated matter* almost to that of a *persona*. But once its connection with my brain became severed, it lost that privileged status, and whether the old wreck lay gutted in a junkyard or rusting peacefully in an Iowa cornfield ceased to matter to me.

The March of the Androids

The illusion of a *spirit* in the machine is heightened, of course, when the machine is given animal or human form and movement. Fascination with such automata goes back many centuries, but reached a height in eighteenth-century France, when clockworks became the power source that drove these creations.

Of all machines, the clockwork has held a special fascination, often being regarded with awe or compassion as though it were a living thing. The poet May Swenson describes a "squint-eyed" watchmaker as he

> undressed my
> watch. I
> watched him
> split her
> in three layers and lay her
> middle—a quivering viscera—in a circle on a little plinth. He
> shoved shirtsleeves up and leaned like an ogre over my
> naked watch.
>
> May Swenson, *The Watch*

The most famous of the builders of such animated figures, or *androids*, as they were frequently called, was Jacques de Vaucanson (1709–1782). His creations include a flute player, a mandolin player that accompanied itself in song, and a duck. Unlike the android-musicians of other mechanists that only pretended to play while a separate music box completed the illusion, Vaucanson's

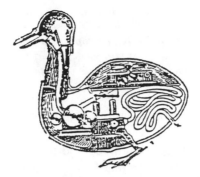

Duck automaton by Jacques de Vaucanson (1709–1782).

puppets really played their instruments. But his best-known creation was a duck that quacked, swam, waddled, ate, and defecated.

Another of the famous *mechanists* of that age was the Baron Wolfgang von Kempelen (1734–1804), who spent many years perfecting an apparatus for producing human speech. He was also the creator of an android, known as The Turk, that he exhibited as a chess-playing automaton. The puppet with the turban was operated, it turned out, by a hidden dwarf who was a master chess player.

If all these attempts appear crude to us now, we must appreciate the profound effect they had on the mentality of the time, to which a sophisticated clockwork represented the cutting edge of technology. This is brought out by a reported church edict in Spain, which threatened with inquisition anyone constructing automata, for fear that the mechanists might uncover the secret of life.

The eighteenth century saw not only the perfection of the machine—mostly in the form of clockworks—but also the emergence of a mechanistic philosophy that interpreted life, including human life, as nothing other than the workings of an intricate mechanism. In the forefront of this movement stood the French philosopher Julien Offray de la Mettrie, who in 1748 published his famous treatise *Man a Machine*, in which he describes man as a kind of self-winding watch. It had a profound and lasting effect. About a century later the Austrian physicist Ludwig Boltzmann echoes la Mettrie with this Germanic sentence:

Only when one admits that
spirit and will are not something over and above the body, but
rather complicated actions of material parts whose ability to
so act becomes increasingly perfected by development, only when

*one admits that intuition, will and self-consciousness are merely
the highest stages of development of these physico-chemical forces
of matter by which primeval protoplasmic bubbles were enabled
to seek regions that were more and avoid those that were less
favorable to them, only then does everything become clear in
psychology.*[2]

And this from Monod, another century later: "The cell is a machine, the animal is a machine. Man is a machine."

Man and machine indeed seemed to edge closer together in the eighteenth century. As machines were made to appear more and more lifelike, humans adopted many of the stereotypic aspects of machines. The minuet and other dances were highly stylized, the gestures, the stiff curtsies, almost mechanical. The costumes and the wigs gave people a puppetlike appearance. Human faces were sometimes hidden behind masks. Some masks with movable parts were used by actors to "increase the range of human expressiveness." But nowhere was the attempt to turn humans into automatons more purposeful and more unrelenting (and perhaps necessary) than in the military. From the uniforms to the lockstep, to the blind obedience, individuality was to be suppressed, or at least made subordinate to a clocklike functioning of a larger whole.

◊◊◊◊

While most of the nineteenth-century scientists still subscribed to a mechanistic interpretation of all life (see Boltzmann's quotation above), popular interest in automata began to decline, and the romantic movement saw in androids not so much objects of wonder as of horror. Representative of that reaction is *The Sandman*, a gothic tale by the German romantic writer E. T. A. Hoffmann. It is the story of a young man who falls in love with Olimpia, whom he believes to be the daughter of his physics professor Spallanzani, but who is really an automaton Spallanzani has contrived with the help of a sinister itinerant peddler named Coppola. The young man is head-over-heels in love with the exceptional beauty of the puppet and even finds a strange attraction in her measured, mechanical movements. Her very limited vocabulary—an occasional "ach, ach" was all she ever managed to say—did not seem to perturb him, which does not say much for the image men of the time had of women. Their expectations clearly were limited.

The reader, however, is made aware of the deception long before the hapless young man suspects anything. When he does find out the truth, he goes mad and commits suicide.

The *robot* is a device that is meant to be more advanced, more *functionally* lifelike, than the automaton. It is a product of the twentieth century, the term "robot" appearing for the first time in a play by the Czech writer Karel Capek,[3] entitled *R.U.R.* The initials stand for "Rossum's Universal Robot." Unlike the wind-up toys of eighteenth-century France, robots are not just curiosities; they carry out tasks, desirable or mischievous.

The contemporary concept of a robot is a flawless machine, dedicated to executing tasks humans can perform only imperfectly. A robot welder will weld faster and more precisely than its human counterpart, and without becoming victim to boredom or fatigue. It will do this without complaint in desert heat or subzero temperatures. A robot soldier would bring his deadly powers without hesitation through a hail of bullets and be impervious to poison gas or biological weapons. But robots, unless they belong to science fiction, are highly specialized machines. A robot welder designed for an automobile factory would not do well in a shipyard.

The modern computer is a different breed of machine. It is a general purpose number cruncher and logic mill. It will analyze the stock market as readily as it computes the orbit of an asteroid. Ask it any question that is computable, any intricate string of syllogisms, and it will give you the answers in the blink of an eye. Load it with massive information, and it will faithfully store it indefinitely, sort it, analyze it, and return it to you when asked. It is the culmination, but certainly not the end, of that long chain of creative processes through which man made matter serve his purposes.

The Indigenous Android and the Promethean Gene

For some time now, one technological objective has been the imitation of life. After such modest beginnings as the androids of the eighteenth-century, we have now succeeded in several instances in surpassing with our machines our own physical and mental faculties.

On the other side of the coin, we observe a dehumanization of man, which may take the form of regimentation of thought and action, of conformism (enforced or desired), all of which makes us act in more predictable, machinelike ways. Some of this conformism is desirable behavior, necessitated by the cooperative venture we call society. Much of it is destructive, limiting our inventiveness and fostering blind obedience to often questionable ends. This mechanistic side is as much part of our makeup as our celebrated ingenuity, independence, and resourcefulness. This tendency to conform, to fall in with the lockstep of the group, to avoid conspicuousness, I will call the *indigenous android (IA)* in us, being the counterpart of *artificial intelligence (AI)*, which is the most humanlike aspect of a machine. We may wonder whether IA and AI are mirror images of each other appearing on opposite sides of a chasm, or adjoining areas in a single continuum. Is there, in other words, a gradual transition between man and machine?

The creative animation with which humans invented and perfected their machines seems simpler at first glance than the evolutionary spontaneous animation from which we emerged, but really is profoundly more complicated. Inventiveness implies *intentionality*, which is the distinguishing feature of *mind*. Characteristically, an end is envisioned, and solutions considered and tested, before actual construction can begin. Much of the testing is carried out through manipulation of images, processes that we will examine more closely in later chapters. There is about creativity an element of unpredictability and impenetrability. It has been suggested that somewhere in our evolutionary past a mutation, called the *Promethean gene*, has given us that creative spark that caused us to diverge so radically from the rest of the animal kingdom.

Can machines be made to follow a similar course? Can the machines we created become, in turn, creators? And would they, like Prometheus, incur the wrath of their own, more powerful, creators, for having overstepped their bounds? We may be creating intelligence, but are we creating *creativity*, or are we, to put it crudely, building more shitting ducks?

The question of the potential powers and limitations of machines is one of the most controversial in science today. The rapidly expanding repertory of these devices is seen as a progressive humanization of the machine, raising questions about possible machine consciousness and machine volition. The arrival of chess-playing computers at world-class level and the ability to prove mathematical theorems by computers are hailed by many as evidence that the gap between man and machine is narrowing.

But we are still looking for our own essence, like Thomas Mann's god when he invented humans. Perhaps we are trying too hard to make machines intelligent. After all, very few humans are world-class chess players, and the majority's mathematical prowess does not exceed grade-school level. Maybe we should search for the essential human qualities at the lowest possible level, that of a man or woman barely emerging out of a coma, following illness or accident, unable to signal with anything but a weak smile or feeble squeeze of hand the recognition of a familiar presence. Could we build a machine to duplicate this simple act? Of course. Would we consider it human? Of course not.

◊◊◊◊

We have pictured the universe as it appeared after the Copernican revolution in the sixteenth century: remote but fascinating, an object of awe to the human mind. The question arose whether provisions for the later appearance of man had been made early in the evolution of the cosmos or whether we stumbled into it as uninvited guests. Either way, the individual human has faced a gap, with him or her on one side and the rest of the universe on the other, the irreducible duality of *I* and *it*.

The evolution of life, which introduced purpose and function into the physical universe, caused a progressive differentiation from the inanimate world, a process that became vastly accelerated when one of the emerging species began to ponder its own relation to the rest of the world.

In a certain sense, the subsequent creative animation carried out by man on his environment reversed this trend. More and more, nature was made to subserve human needs and fancies, the planet was *humanized*, and finally even outer space became our playground. We have turned our radio telescopes on distant stars, expecting to find evidence there of something resembling human intelligence.

Our latest technological creations have blurred the distinction between man and machine. The efforts of the eighteenth-century French makers of automata may seem primitive to us now, but their androids were the forerunners of today's high-tech robots, and their feats were quite as remarkable then as those of today's supercomputers. And the question was asked then as now: What, if anything, is missing in these machines to make them human?

To answer this question we must try to understand how mind arises in the machinery of the human brain. To this end we will examine the flow of information through a sensory system—our sense of vision—and observe how the brain turns events seen into images, and images into thoughts, and thoughts back into images.

I will propose that the mechanism I call the *creative loop*, a cycle of self-referent neural activity, can be made to account for the so-called *higher brain functions*. We will return to the question of a machine's ability to mimic man. There is the question, finally, whether—by an act of creative animation—we might be able to start a cycle of spontaneous evolution of systems or *creatures* that may be called alive.

PART TWO

BODY AND MIND

The eye is not satisfied with seeing,
nor the ear filled with hearing.

Eccelesiastes 1:8

Chapter 5

McCulloch's Query: Why the Mind Is in the Head

When we think hard, we often touch palm to forehead as though to comfort the hardworking organ behind it, and we sometimes shake our heads as if to clear the brain of accumulated wastes and shake it into activity. We take our mind's being there so much for granted that most of us would readily testify that we have a direct sensation of the brain working. But we think we *feel* our thoughts emanating from our head only because we are told that's where they are bred. The brain, which is the crossroads of all our sensations, in fact has no sensation of itself.

Definitive notions of brain mechanisms, based on the known characteristics of individual neurons, began to take shape in the 1940s. They were inspired by two contemporaneous scientific developments: the rapid advances in computer technology, and a breakthrough in instrumentation that made it possible to observe the activity of single neurons in a functioning brain.

Neurons were found to communicate with each other not unlike the on/off elements in a computer exchanging signals between them. This analogy led to the conceptualization of the brain as a gigantic network of nearly identical and multiply interconnected units; it was called the *neural net*. The staggering complexity of this organ became a powerful argument for "why the mind is in the head." In 1943, in a celebrated paper, the psychiatrist Warren McCulloch, with the help of a mathematician, Walter Pitts, showed that such a neural net could carry out any describable logical function. The authors optimistically state that "both the formal and the final aspects of that activity which we are wont to call *mental* are rigorously deducible from present neurophysiology." They further conclude that "the psychiatrist may take comfort from the obvious conclusion concerning causality—that, for prognosis, history is never necessary."[1] It is important to understand fully all that is implied in the last statement. Everything that affects your brain in the next instant is contained in the *state* of your brain at this instant. Causality is local in space and time. It does not jump over gaps. The present state, if only it were known precisely, tells us everything we want to know about the future.

◊◊◊◊

The brain's imperial role within the body has been recognized almost since the beginning of recorded history, with the exception of some notable lapses: the Homeric heroes thought with their diaphragms, and Aristotle, who has misled us on so many things, convinced people for centuries after him that thinking was done by the heart.

We find the brain first mentioned in an ancient Egyptian manuscript known as the Edwin Smith papyrus, whose author is believed to have been a surgeon who lived around 3000 B.C. Among the surgical case histories described in the document is a detailed account of a head injury in which the brain was exposed. It appears evident that the author realized the role of the brain as the seat of sensations and bodily control.[2]

Alcmaeon of Croton, rather than Hippocrates, is often called the father of Greek medicine. He lived in the fifth century B.C. and is believed to have been a disciple of Pythagoras. He had performed surgery on the eye, discovered the optic nerve, and taught that the brain was the central receiving organ of all our senses. Then, almost two centuries after him, Aristotle, in one of his major blunders, announced that thinking is done in the heart, and that the brain served merely to cool the blood and prevent the heart from overheating.

It was Hippocrates who introduced the theory of four *humors*, fluids whose mix determined the mood as well as the physical well-being of a person, thus foreshadowing contemporary brain chemistry. Six centuries later, the Greco-Roman physician Galen elaborated on the humor theory. Brain mechanisms, to Galen, were a matter of hydrodynamics, with the humors streaming through the various cavities, or *ventricles*, of the brain. The idea remained popular throughout the Middle Ages.

But Aristotle's old notion about the heart was far from dead. "Tell me where is fancy bred, or in the heart or in the head?" asks Shakespeare in *The Merchant of Venice*, and Galileo in the beginning of the seventeenth century still finds it necessary to argue that the brain must be the organ of control, since so many more nerves originate and terminate there than at the heart.

Still, the brain has never been an organ that elicited much popular attention, especially when compared with that glamor-hogging fist-sized muscle in your chest. There is still the powerful popular notion today that we know things *in our hearts* that the analytic brain simply fails to understand, and the suitor who tells his beloved that he loves her with all his brain is likely to be rejected as a heartless fellow.

The progressively critical, we may call it *scientific*, approach to brain study is shown in the juxtaposition of drawings spanning a period of less than half a century. The first is a famous and much-copied drawing by the monk Gregor Reisch (1467–1525). It is more symbolic than representative, expressing the then current views about brain function, derived to a large extent from Galen. The convolutions of the solid part of the brain merit only a few symbolic swirls that clearly express the artist's view of their insignificance.

The ventricles dominate the picture. The most forward of these is labeled *sensus communis*. It was believed that the information gathered by all the senses converges there, to be mixed with imagination and fantasy. Our expression *common sense* is derived from that old notion of a single, common sensorium. (In modern neuroscience this has been replaced by many so-called *sensory association areas*.)

From the first ventricle the information-laden fluid is filtered, according to Reisch's drawing, through a narrow passage, the *vermis*, and passes to the next cavity, where cognition and thought take place. Another narrow passage leads to the storage area labeled *memorativa*.

Leonardo da Vinci, a contemporary of Reisch, clearly was influenced by the doctrines then current. Unlike his other masterful anatomical drawings, his portrayal of the human brain is like a cartoon. Not even swirls dignify the neural mass he must have seen in his dissections. The cranial vault is empty except for three ventricles that are like bubbles floating in the void.

The third drawing is by the Belgian anatomist Andreas Vesalius. His monumental treatise *De humani corporis fabrica* appeared

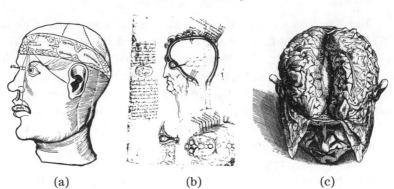

(a)   (b)   (c)

Three drawings of the human brain: (a) *Gregor Reisch;* (b) *Leonardo da Vinci;* (c) *Andreas Vesalius.*

in the year 1543, the same year in which Copernicus published his revolutionary book on the motion of the heavenly bodies. Vesalius's work was revolutionary in its own right. In his numerous careful drawings of all aspects of the brain, he does not attempt to express a particular theory of function, but approaches the living form with the unbiased curiosity of a true anatomist. We see here the first portrayal of the brain that looks like a brain.

The notion that fluids coursing through the cerebral ventricles carry out the complex functions of perception, association, memory, recall, and thought finally was replaced by the realization that the brain's activities took place not in the fluid-filled cavities but in the convoluted, solid matter that both Reisch and Leonardo overlooked. Not until near the end of the nineteenth century did scientists realize that the brain consists of highly specialized cells, the *neurons,* whose fibers with their prolific branches link with one another and form a network so vast and so dense that it seems all but hopeless to try to unravel it. According to current estimates, about 200 billion such cells exist in the human head, in addition to a trillion or so other cell types.

What, then, is the function of the ventricles that are embedded in this neural mass? The cerebrospinal fluid they contain is not the carrier of memories and thoughts. For a while it was believed to be nothing more than a kind of cerebral sewer system, carrying away waste products. We now know that it also brings in nutrients and may be the carrier of chemical messengers.

Again, old theories don't go away easily. The fluid theory lives on in modern Freudian psychiatry, which tells us that unwanted memories that are suppressed will cause dangerous pressures to build up in the psyche, and must—like an incompressible fluid that is pushed back—pop up somewhere else. This image, although based on totally false premises, has such powerful intuitive appeal that it is considered virtually self-evident. One gathers from it, through seemingly irrefutable logic, that painful experiences must never be allowed to subside on their own, let alone be pushed into the background, but must be *vented*—talked about, rehashed—after which they will rise in the air above the psychiatrist's couch like a flock of departing blackbirds. Opponents have derisively called Freudian theory *psychohydraulics* and pointed out that it is a throwback to Galen.

❦❦❦❦

I have before me a set of pictures of slices through a human brain that look very much like the drawings Vesalius made four and a half centuries ago. I can trace out the convolutions of the cerebral cortex, the underlying white matter, and all the subcortical structures, such as the thalamus, the corpus callosum, the pons, the amygdala, and the cerebellum. The pictures show horizontal and vertical slices through the brain that expose every one of its features.

Somewhere in the recesses of this labyrinth—perhaps in microstructures so small that only a powerful microscope could reveal them—or perhaps distributed over all of it, somewhere, somehow, this neural machinery contains a *self*, a conscious mind.

"I know him, Horatio," I mutter, as I replace the sheets of film in a large manila envelope that has my name on it. I have been contemplating my own brain, made accessible painlessly, noninvasively, through the technique of magnetic resonance imaging (MRI).

The machinery of the brain differs in many respects fundamentally from any machine we have built. Perhaps most obvious is the fact that for machines we have blueprints. We designed them. We understand them. In the case of the brain, not only is our knowledge of its structure rudimentary, we also have a poor understanding of many of its functions. Another difference lies in the specificity of machine functions compared with the bewildering variety of disparate tasks carried out by the brain. It controls body temperature and blood acidity; it dispenses the right balance of hormones, controls our growth when we are young, and stops it when we are adults; it initiates our aging processes, and—unless some other calamity befalls us first—it probably programs and executes our eventual demise. These are only some of the many so-called *autonomic* functions of the brain.

Its most conspicuous features, however, have to do with its interaction with the outside world. It gathers a steady stream of information by way of our senses and provides appropriate responses via our muscles. Our concern in this book will be limited mostly to the portion that is sometimes called the *sensorimotor* brain. Here we discern two distinct modes of operation. In one, sensory messages are rapidly sifted and a predetermined motor response is released. The knee-jerk is one of the simplest of these *reflexes*; another is the pupillary reflex, in which the iris of the eye automatically adjusts to varying levels of illumination. Some reflexes involve learning, but once acquired, they are just as spontaneous. You will, without hesitation, hit the brake of your car when a pedestrian steps off the curb in front of you. In all these cases the reaction follows the stimulus by no more than a few tenths of a second, and the entire reflex may be thought of as a one-way passage of signals from sensors to muscles.

In a different mode of operation, which we may call *thinking*, considerable time may elapse between stimulus and action. We must assume that nervous activity in the brain persists for seconds or longer. And because nerve signals travel quite fast from one part of the brain to another, we conclude that information is shuffled and shuttled back and forth between different brain centers before the matter is resolved.

Chapter 6

The Nuts and Bolts of Mind

"I," you say, and are proud
of the word. But greater is that in which you do not wish
to have faith—your body and its great reason: that does
not say "I," but does I.

F. Nietzsche, *Thus Spoke Zarathustra*

The Senses

There is an old saying that nothing is in the mind that did not
earlier come through the senses. To understand *thinking* we therefore must understand what happens in our sensory apparatus. In
humans, the dominant sense is vision. It is not surprising, therefore, that a large part of the vast field of neuroscience is devoted
to the study of the various neural structures that link the eye to
the higher brain centers. Our knowledge of the structure and function of all parts of this *visual pathway* is still incomplete but more
extensive than that of any other part of the brain.

We do understand machines because we designed and built
them. A common approach to vision is therefore to look at some
man-made systems that do similar things: the photographic camera
and the video camera. Let us then approach vision by using the
metaphor of machine *data acquisition*, and see how far we can get.

Cameras, just like our visual pathways, begin with an optical
lens that takes the light rays coming from the objects in front of
us and forms an *image* in the focal plane. The concept of an image
has to be made clear. What we are talking about is a concentration
of light distributed over a surface in such a way that—*if we were
to look at it*—we would get the impression of looking at the objects
themselves.

In the still camera, a piece of light-sensitive material, the film,
is located in the focal plane of the lens. With the momentary

opening of the shutter, the incoming light pattern causes chemical changes in the film, the latent image, which after development forms the real image we call the *picture*. It is really only a record of the light pattern formed by the lens, a distribution of grains of silver or pigment. It becomes an image or picture only when viewed by a human who, by some neural processes yet to be unraveled, associates that motionless scattering of pigment grains with a live scenery.

The movie camera does more. It takes stills in such rapid succession that, when they are reprojected, the form and motion we perceive seem so real that they can make us laugh or cry. Again, without the human viewer, the movie is just a strip of plastic.

The video camera is one of our most recent visual data acquisition systems. Again, a lens forms a real image that is now electronically *scanned*, and the response is coded sequentially on a magnetic tape. When replayed through a television set, an electron beam sweeps rapidly across the face of the viewing screen, exciting phosphors to blink on briefly as the beam passes over them. At any given moment only one small spot on the screen is thus excited; others are just dying out from having been excited moments earlier; still others are dark. The picture is put together by the human visual system and the rest of the brain, through which the parts that exist at different instances are integrated and perceived as a moving scene. Evidently, a fair amount of sophistication is involved in this process, since animals that have visual pathways very similar to ours seem unimpressed by movies or TV. Something very subtle must be happening in the brain after the *data acquisition*.

The emergence of computer technology in the last few decades seemed to provide insight. In computers, *raw* data acquire meaning through elaborate transformations in which facts are regrouped, comparisons made with stored data, and features analyzed and extracted. On the basis of all this *information processing*, conclusions can be drawn and decisions can be made. The computer also may be attached to systems of levers and switches that control and operate mechanical systems. In every modern automobile, a computer, informed by sensors of the current status, thus controls vital functions of the engine. It is not surprising that such computers are called the *brains* of the machinery they control.

By the same analogy, we try to understand the transformation of the light images formed on the retina into perception, conscious recognition, and decision making, by thinking of the brain as a computer interposed between the sensors and our muscles. This computer metaphor is currently the favorite tool in interpreting brain function.

The metaphor is reinforced further by a similarity in the actions of the on/off logic elements of a computer and the neurons that make up the brain. Both are *binary* elements, that is, they have two possible output states: zero or one in the case of the computer, active or nonactive in case of the neuron. This so-called *all-or-none* action of the neuron is somewhat of an oversimplification, but it has been made the basis of numerous brain models. We take a closer look now at the neural machinery to explore further the computer metaphor of the brain.

Neurons

The *neuron* is the key to understanding what the brain does and how it does it. We want to look briefly at its structure and function because, to a first approximation, that's all the brain is: neurons—vast numbers of them. There are also other types of cells, the *glial* cells, even more numerous than the neurons. These are generally believed to play only a supportive role, but we may yet be in for some surprises here. The rest of the brain is blood vessels, the already mentioned ventricles, and massive fiber bundles that connect the neurons. To the best of our knowledge, thinking is the business of the neurons.

The question of whether the individual neuron can feel, decide, think, is immediately raised. The term *gnostic neuron* has been used to describe this. Some physiologists have speculated that there might be a single neuron that can be said to be the nerve center, the true *I*, the ultimate arbiter, the *pontifical neuron*, as it was called. But it is more commonly thought that these functions somehow are distributed over populations of neurons. We are getting ahead of the story, however.

What is a neuron? It is a living cell, with a cell body enclosed in a membrane, a nucleus, cytoplasm, and all the other equipment most other cells possess. It differs from other cells in two respects: The cell body has lengthy protrusions, fibers that branch out in different directions and are the cables through which messages are sent and received. This is made possible by the second feature peculiar to neurons: The membranes enclosing these fibers are *excitable*, which means that they can carry signals in the form of electrical impulses.

The fibers are of two distinct types: the *dendrites*, which, like shrubs, have many stems emanating from the body of the cell, each one branching further repeatedly; and the single *axon*, rising like a tree trunk from the cell before it too branches out. A neuron receives signals through the shrubbery of its dendrites, and passes information to other neurons by way of its axon tree. The information consists of electrical signals that travel along the fibers of a neuron, and chemical messengers that are passed from one neuron to others. On the input (dendrite) side of the neuron, the electrical signals are called *post-synaptic potentials* (PSPs). The output, or response, of the neuron travels along the axon and all of its branches and is called the *action potential*. It is here that the neuron exhibits its all-or-none character. The action potential is a brief electrical pulse of standard height. When it appears, we say the neuron *fires*.

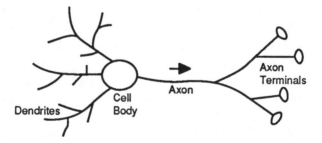

Schematic diagram of a neuron. The arrow marks the direction of information flow.

The axon branches of a neuron generally connect to other neurons, although some go directly to muscles or glands and thus are part of the *output* of the nervous system. The axon terminals make junctions called *synapses*. Most of these consist of a narrow gap separating the axon terminal of one neuron from a dendrite of another. The diagram below shows a neuron drawn more realistically, including cell body, dendrites, and axon with its branches and terminals. Axon terminals from other neurons (dotted) are shown making synapses on the dendrites of a neuron. The inset shows a much enlarged picture of a synapse, with the axon terminal, a bulblike structure above, and parts of the dendrite of the receiving cell below.

Communication across the synaptic gap is by chemical messengers, special molecules called *neurotransmitters* that are released by the axon terminal and diffuse across the gap. When reaching the dendrite, they produce the post-synaptic potentials. The sum of all the post-synaptic potentials coming in from all the dendrites and arriving at the cell body at any given time will determine whether that cell will, in turn, produce an action potential.

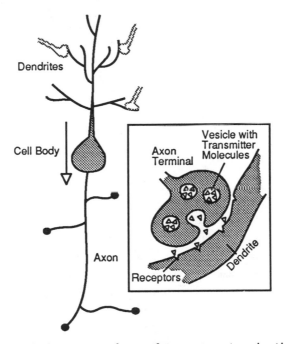

A neuron with three axons from other neurons terminating on its dendrites and cell body. Inset: greatly enlarged synapse, showing axon terminal, receiving cell.

Here is the entire sequence of events by which neurons communicate with each other: A given neuron may have many thousands of synapses distributed over its field of dendrites, producing a steady rain of post-synaptic potentials to descend on the cell body. When the combined effect of this bombardment exceeds a certain value, the *threshold*, the cell responds with an action potential of its own, which now travels, like a wave, outward along its axon and to all of the axon terminals. The neuron *fires*. The output is *binary*, all or none, zero or one, which is so suggestive of logic units in a digital computer. Through its outgoing synapses it produces post-synaptic potentials on other neurons.

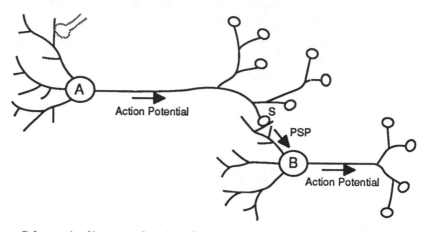

Schematic diagram showing the sequence of events in the triggering of a neuron (B) by a neuron (A). An action potential in (A) causes transmitter molecules to be released at a synapse S. The resulting PSP contributes to the emission of action potential by neuron (B).

That each neuron has an input (the post-synaptic potentials) and an output (the action potential) is a fundamental fact that is not stressed often enough. The output either serves to communicate with other neurons or to send a signal to a muscle or a gland. No neuron is just a receiver or ultimate destination of information. It serves only to pass it on. Therefore we should not consider individual neurons as *knowing* or *understanding* anything. The *gnostic* neuron and the *pontifical* neuron are concepts that don't conform to biological reality. Similarly, we must assume that even those neurons whose activity has been shown to represent the detection of specific sensory patterns—the so-called *feature analyzers*—cannot be said to have anything like a knowledge that the feature is present. They function merely as links in the chain that leads to cognition. But if every neuron is just an intermediary unit, where does cognition actually take place?

Time is an important and frequently unappreciated element in brain function. The firing of a neuron is a process that occupies about one-thousandth of a second. That is as long as the action potential lasts when observed anywhere along the axon. But because of the limited speed with which the signal is propagated, it will appear at different times at the various axon terminals. At the synapses, there is a further delay between the arrival of the action potential and the post-synaptic potentials appearing on the receiving cell membrane. This *synaptic delay* is also about one-thousandth of a second. Thus the time that passes between the firing of a cell and its effect on the next cell will be due partly to the delay at the synapse. Another delay is caused by the time it takes the action potential to travel down the axon from the cell body to the axon terminal. That time depends on the length of the path and the speed with which the signals propagate along the axon.

A given sensory message—seeing the approach of an automobile, for example—therefore will arrive at different times at different brain centers. And a given center may receive the same or equivalent messages via different routes, hence at different times. A neural message also may reverberate for a time, bouncing back and forth between two brain centers like an echo. I mention this to bring out the fact that what happens in the world of objects in one moment translates into neural events that are distributed in time. This *temporal divergence* has an analog in the spatial domain. *Spatial divergence* means that a stimulus in the visual field, such as a point of light, causes neural activity that again is distributed and will generally overlap activity caused by a different point stimulus. This mixing of events in both space and time is of crucial significance in cognition, which is the extraction of valuable information from the "raw" sense data.

The Neural Net

In the human brain, approximately 100 billion neurons form an intricate network, tightly interconnected through trillions of synapses. The famous Oxford neurophysiologist Charles Sherrington called this the *enchanted loom*. All of these neurons are present at birth, as well as many more that are later pruned away during early development. No new neurons will be formed for the rest of our lives. To reach this number by the time we are born, neurons must be generated throughout our nine months of embryonic development at the prodigious rate of close to five thousand per second!

In the mature brain, a single neuron may be in communication with thousands of others at the same time. It is as though 100 billion people—twenty times the world's human population—were simultaneously chattering away and listening over telephone lines that connected each to as many as thousands of others at the same time. But that is not all. Not only do neurons listen to the information that comes across their private lines (the synapses from other neurons), they also *hear* announcements coming over a cerebral public address system consisting of chemical messengers that are *broadcast* through the bloodstream. This *volume transmission* of chemical flavors,[1] which are not unlike Galen's humors, is believed to be responsible for the communication of such general brain states as mood, affect, biological cycle, sexual arousal, and degree of alertness and attention. Again, no neuron is a terminal receiver. It listens and hears only to pass the information on.

The term *neural net* suggests a broad connectivity between neurons. Almost any part of the brain is connected—directly or indirectly—to any other part. But there are also distinctly sequential structures or *neural pathways*. These are avenues of neural traffic that crisscross the nervous system. The *auditory pathway*, for example, comprises many neurons that convey the information picked up by the inner ear along a string of *relay stations* to the cerebral cortex. Similarly, there is a *visual pathway*, and pathways for all other senses. Then there are pathways that lead from the cortex *down* to our muscles, the *motor pathways*.

Up and Down: Sensors and Effectors

Putting together the incoming sensory and outgoing motor pathways, we arrive at a quite plausible picture of what the brain does. It seems to function as the computer that sifts and analyzes what is received by the senses and comes up with appropriate responses. In this sensorimotor paradigm of brain function we can describe arcs through the nervous system, leading from sensation to action.

The figure below is a sketch of the brain centers and their interconnections that conforms to this picture of the sensorimotor brain. We see the visual pathway that leads from the eye to a part in the cortex called *visual cortex*, or *V1*. From another part of the cortex, the *motor cortex*, fibers descend to the muscles.

Another structure is important to our discussion. Located in a region called the *thalamus* are *sensory relays*, or way stations between the senses and the cortex. One of these is the visual relay,

Cortex

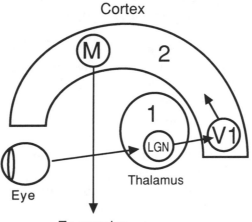

Parts of the sensorimotor brain, *showing the thalamus (1) with LGN and the cerebral cortex (2) with the visual cortex, V1. The arrows show* ascending *visual information and* descending *pathways from cortex to muscles.*

which has the anatomical name *lateral geniculate nucleus*, or *LGN*. Remember the name *LGN* and its location. It plays a big role in the story I am telling, and I will refer to it often.

We mentioned *arcs* of neural activity going from sensors to muscles. The simplest such arcs are the spinal reflexes, such as the *knee jerk*. A tap below the kneecap is picked up by special sensors that connect directly to neurons that trigger the muscle response. We can do very little to prevent this response.

Other reflexes are more complex, that is, they go through higher brain centers and involve larger numbers of neurons, some of which are affected by other stimuli. The reflex thus may be conditional: If *A* happens, respond with *X*, unless *B* happens also. Still, reflexes are characterized by the speed with which even complex responses are triggered by sensory inputs. In a fencing match, seeing the opponent's thrust will be processed rapidly through the nervous system, causing the muscles to perform a parry. The tennis player will observe the approaching ball and carry out the appropriate body motions for a successful return.

It is tempting to view all cerebral decision making, indeed all *behavior*, as just a more elaborate form of this primitive paradigm of a reflex. It could be argued that the only difference between a knee jerk and, say, formulating a reasoned response to a question is the greater number of neural systems intervening between

the sensors and effectors, allowing one to *learn* appropriate reflexes and, as occasion demands, modify or interdict the learned
response.

I question the usefulness of this approach. The latter form of
behavior, because of the longer times involved, must require more
than neural activity being conducted through a simple arc. This
follows from the speed with which neural impulses are conducted
and the relatively small number of synaptic links leading from sensors to effectors. Any process that we may associate with *thinking*
must therefore involve sustained, circulatory neural activity quite
different from the one-way conduction along a reflex *arc*.

The sensory stimuli, on reaching the central nervous system,
generally pass through a number of stages of *processing*. Similarly,
we can discern different levels on the efferent, or motor, side.
Again, the sensory information is pictured as going *up* toward
higher and higher levels, and the motor commands are said to
descend toward the motoneurons that activate our muscles. The
region in between these two, the cerebral cortex, becomes more
diffuse and confusing as we move away from the two peripheries.

S and R

The school of psychology known as *behaviorism* would consider the outcome of any set of stimuli at any one time to be just
as rigidly and deterministically tied to the stimuli as the knee jerk
is to the knee tap. Behaviorists also contend that the stimuli at
one end of the sensorimotor arc and the response at the other are
the only truly observable features of brain activity. All the intervening phenomena, such as motivation, volition, or *thinking*, can
never be objects of scientific investigation, because they cannot
be observed except through unreliable and unverifiable introspection. It is best, therefore, to leave these concepts out of considera-
tion altogether. This is also called the *stimulus-response*, or *S-R*,
approach: Instead of the previous figure, a black box with two
arrows now represents the brain. It may be doing very complicated
and unobservable things, but we can observe only the entering
stimuli (*S*) and the emerging responses (*R*). Behaviorist psychology
is the art of relating the two without attempting to see what is
inside the box.

The S-R approach has yielded much interesting information
but lost much of its earlier popularity. It is useless in situations

where stimulus and response are not immediately and evidently linked. The psychologist Jerome Bruner refers to the *"impeccable peripheralism"* of behavioral theory. Consider, for example, the actions of an artist or a writer. We cannot account for their work as simple responses to sets of stimuli unless we include among them many previous experiences—reading, studying, perhaps the experiences of a lifetime. There is little connection between present behavior and whatever stimuli happen to be around at the time. To the writer or the composer at work, sensory stimulation is only distraction. Their behavior cannot be explained by anything an outsider might observe. We must look at the brain as *creating* something out of its own cloth, so to speak (see (*b*) in the diagram).

The opposite situation would be equally baffling to the behavioral psychologist. Consider a situation in which a massive amount of information is pouring in through our senses but produces no significant observable response: a person is listening to a lecture or to a piece of music, or contemplating a painting, or reading, or watching TV. The absence of stimulus-connected behavior does not signify that the stimulus is disregarded. On the contrary, we *know* that very significant processes must take place inside the brain, but they are inaccessible to the strict behaviorist.

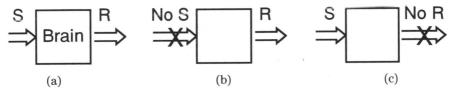

(a) (b) (c)

The sensorimotor brain: (a) full stimulus-response (S-R) function; (b) response without stimulus; (c) stimulus without response.

The ultimate puzzle is depicted in the diagram below. Here, both stimulation and behavior are largely absent. The person's attention is directed inward. His mental activities have very little to do with what goes on around him. He is *thinking.* "Thinking?" the behaviorist might say. "I see only a naked man sitting on a rock holding his head."

Searching for the Pinnacle

In our preoccupation with the machinery of the nervous system, we seem to have lost sight of the mind. If there is an *I,* where in this neural maze must we look for it? Intuition tells us that we must follow the lowly peripheral pathways upward toward what are considered the *highest* brain centers. But what is the highest? Will we perhaps find at the very pinnacle of this neural pyramid a single neuron, the already mentioned pontifical neuron?

The isolated brain. (Nothing comes in, nothing goes out.)

But searching for such a center among the many billion neurons is like being lost in a rain forest. All we find is more trees. We soon lose any sense of what is up or down in this green hell of neural fibers and conclude that there is no such thing as a real center or pinnacle. Perhaps the notion of a conscious self, hidden somewhere in all this, is also illusory. Perhaps we are really little more than automata, designed to produce the right response for every stimulus. But then the thinker who sees nothing and does nothing would be a nonfunctioning human being.

In the next chapter we shall see that the diagram on page 53, although correct as far as it goes, has omitted some very important features: neural pathways that seem to go the wrong way and therefore have been largely ignored by most neurophysiologists.

Artificial Nets

Neurons, as we have seen, act like individual switches that are turned on when input from other, similar switches exceeds a certain threshold. The simplicity of this concept has inspired theoreticians to study networks of similar, *electronic* devices, or to simulate such networks using computers. The objective here is twofold: First, the dynamics of such *artificial nets* may yield insight into the behavior of their real, biological counterparts. Second, it is hoped that devices of this kind may be able to solve some specific engineering problems. Also, more farfetched, there is the supposition by some that the artificial devices may not only simulate intelligent function but may be called intelligent in their own right.

This brings up the question of whether there is an intrinsic boundary between life, on the one hand, and the embodiments of creative animation, our machines, on the other.

Work on neural nets began in the 1940s and received a big boost in 1943, when the psychiatrist Warren McCulloch in collaboration with the mathematician Walter Pitts published their theoretical paper showing that a network of neuronlike elements can carry out any logical function that we can define.[2] Later, Frank Rosenblatt of Cornell University proposed a simple network consisting of layers of artificial neurons.[3] These so-called *perceptrons* included a layer of input neurons, a layer of output neurons, and one or more layers of "hidden" units in between. As the diagram shows, information flows in one direction only, from bottom to top. There are no loops.

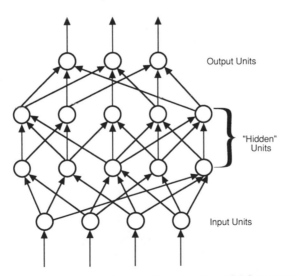

Output Units

"Hidden" Units

Input Units

A perceptron. Input goes to a layer of input units, which connect to layers of "hidden" units and eventually to output units as shown. The one-way connections between pairs of units are of different strengths and are subjected to training.

The perceptron is *trained* in a series of instructional steps in which the strengths of the signals from one unit to another are adjusted depending on whether the output units show the desired "answer."

Perceptrons were shown to perform a number of interesting tasks, such as pattern recognition, but after 1969, when Minsky and Papert demonstrated some of the inherent limitations,[4] interest in perceptrons faded, and virtually no further work was done for the next fifteen years. Other efforts concentrated on neural nets which contained loops and feedbacks. Unlike the *feed-forward* perceptrons, such general nets have more interesting properties but are much more difficult to study.[5]

Recently there has been a revival of interest in both types of artificial neural nets, and again, with more sophisticated structures at hand, the question of just how intelligent such devices can become is raised.

Chapter 7

Vision:
Early Processing

Our casual survey of brain structure in the last chapter has not turned up evidence for the existence anywhere of a command center or of a small group of neurons that could be identified with a quintessential *I*. There is neural traffic that can justifiably be called *up*, and other signal flow just as clearly leading *down*. There are peripheral areas of the brain and so-called *higher* centers. But, unlike a pyramid, the brain opens up into vaster regions the higher we go in our explorations. Eventually, we find ourselves going both up and down, as well as sideways, and the image of having lost our way in a rain forest becomes vivid again.

Let us start with an excursion along a sensory pathway, beginning at the peripheral sensors, until we lose ourselves in the maze of the cerebral cortex. We choose vision for our exploratory journey, because sight is the principal window through which humans apprehend the world. What we believe most is what we see, and most of our thoughts and dreams are visionary. The trip will prove worthwhile, because we will encounter some unexpected surprises along the way.

We begin with the pattern of light that the lens of the eye projects onto the retina, much like the pattern of light a camera lens throws on a piece of photographic film. In the camera this light pattern creates a distribution of pigment grains on a piece of film. I pointed out that this should not properly be called an *image* unless perceived through the human visual system. We now face the problem of where along the visual pathway this transformation of just-pattern into image takes place. Where, in other words, do we recognize and become aware of what we are seeing?

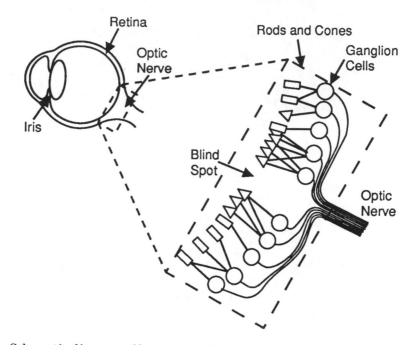

Schematic diagram of human eye showing iris, lens, retina, and optic nerve. Inset: section of retina with rods and cones. (Note: the positions of sensors and retinal ganglion cells are reversed here for clarity.)

Light does not travel trough brain tissue, but electrical signals do. The first task of the visual system is therefore to translate the patterns of light formed by the lens into patterns of electrical activity of neurons. In the retina, light is focused on a sheet of sensors that, by chemical action, amplify the light energy received by a factor of about a hundred thousand and converts it into electrical impulses. The two types of such sensors are called *rods* and *cones*.

The visual pathway can be pictured as a series of interconnected sheets of cells, the first of which is the layer of rods and cones in the retina. There are several more layers of neurons in the retina. From the last of these, the optic nerve carries the messages to more sheets of cells located in the thalamus, the already mentioned visual relay called LGN.

At first, the pattern of neural activities is very similar to the light pattern projected on the retina. If we could see the neurons flashing on and off in the retina or the LGN, we would discern an *image*, a picture of the scene we are looking at. Since we can't, we must relegate perception to higher centers along the visual pathway.

The *pattern* of activities is transmitted by the optic nerve from the retina to the LGN, and from there to V1 in the cortex. The original pattern is more or less maintained as the visual information is relayed from one center to the next. But all sorts of transformations and corrective operations are carried out along the way. Some coding—to represent properties peculiar to light, such as color—also takes place.

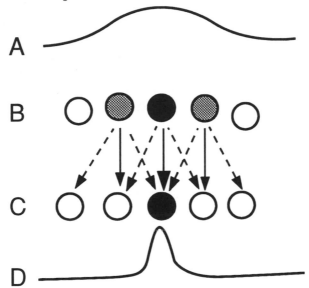

Lateral inhibition. A fuzzy pattern (A), *represented by neural activities* (B), *is sharpened through lateral inhibition (dotted arrows). The resulting activities* (C) *show a sharper contour* (D).

An important process in virtually all sensory processing is called *lateral inhibition*. Through sideways connections that inhibit rather than excite (dotted arrows), a fuzzy pattern may be changed into one having sharp outlines.

These early stages of processing are often referred to as *mappings*, because the patterns remain essentially intact. They have been improved in certain respects, fuzziness reduced and edges sharpened. But beyond the visual cortex (V1), neural activities are transformed in such a way that they no longer would be recognizable as images of the real world *even if we could look at them.*

Up the Visual Pathway

Following the visual pathway into the cerebral cortex reveals a number of neural centers, each specialized to be sensitive to particular features of the incoming sensory pattern. The processes occurring at these higher levels are often understood as *feature extraction*. By this we mean that certain neural circuits are designed to become active when the scene contains specific features. A feature extractor for the color red would become active when the scene contains red objects. Other feature extractors may be specific to certain simple shapes, others to motion, still others to faces.

Traveling farther *upward* along the visual pathway, we find that purely visual information now becomes mixed with similarly processed signals that have arrived via the auditory, tactile, or another sensory pathway. The memory of past experiences, recalled through associations, will add further to the content of the sensory messages. We are now deep in the neural jungle, and most of what is said about this part is controversial. If we went much farther, we would get into centers concerned with the output of the brain, the so-called *descending* pathways that innervate our muscles.

The process of feature extraction actually starts in V1, where it was first discovered by the Harvard neurophysiologists David Hubel and Torsten Wiesel, for which they received the Nobel prize. The features extracted there are relatively simple, mostly lines or edges of specific orientation.

On the principle that there are no terminal or gnostic neurons, the extraction of features by one group of cells should not be considered recognition of that feature, but serves only to signal its presence to some other nerve center.

Anyone trying to understand perception is now faced with this dilemma: The light pattern that was projected onto the retina, and its early neural representations, contained in one location all the information we wish to extract. In the course of processing through the cortical visual centers, the pattern is dissembled and different features are expressed symbolically in different locations.

The English neurobiologist Semir Zeki points out that areas V1 and V2 in the cortex (see diagram on page 65), which receive all visual information from the LGN, "act as a kind of post office parceling out different signals" to the higher cortical areas.[1] One of these, V3, is said to be concerned with dynamic form, V4 extracts information on color, and V5 is sensitive to motion but insensitive to color. However, the high degree of fine spatial detail that exists at retina, LGN, and V1 is largely lost in the higher centers.

Thus, if a woman in a red dress were to move across your field of vision, there would be appropriate activity in the region V3 where form is detected; in the region V4, which contains feature extractors for color; and in the region V5, which is sensitive to motion. We look in vain for a center where all these bits of information are reassembled into a perceptual whole. The woman in the red dress has disappeared and is replaced by a variety of coded symbols that are scattered over different parts of the brain.

Scrambling of the original pattern may be said to take place in time as well as in space. Because of the different travel times of the signals as they go from one level to the next, time is distorted, earlier events may appear later, and vice versa. It may even be said that *future* events affect present neural activity, because the brain—joyfully or fearfully—anticipates, projects into, the future.

As to the pattern of neural activity at these higher centers, its coherence and fidelity to objective reality has been lost and seems to be beyond our power to recoup, at least in the standard view of the visual pathway as a one-way sequence of sequential processing. Patterns have been replaced by neural cryptograms we can no longer read. It now appears a hopeless task to transform these high-level neural messages into an image of the scene before us.

The philosopher Daniel Dennett speaks of *multiple drafts* of a scene being attended to by hordes of homunculi, each knowing and doing different things. "All varieties of perception—indeed, all varieties of thought or mental activity—are accomplished in the brain by parallel, multitrack processes of interpretation and elaboration of sensory inputs," states Dennett.[2]

Is there a place where it all comes together again? The neurologist Antonio Damasio of the University of Iowa, finds that "there is no neuroanatomical structure in the cerebral cortex to which signals from all the sensory modalities that may be represented in our experience can converge, spatially and temporally."[3]

In an attempt to understand the transformations performed by the various neural centers in the visual pathway, scientists have devised the so-called *computational approach*.[4] The operations carried out are aptly named *sensory information processing*. It is the function of the system to *compute* important facts from the data given. In the computational approach, the original light pattern is the cryptogram, and the results of the computations appear, in coded form, at the various higher brain centers. The theory also implies that the path from vision to perception consists of a series of logical steps that could be implemented on a real computer if they were known in detail, with clear implications for the pursuit of artificial intelligence.

The computational approach raises a number of disturbing questions. If the firing of a given neuron or group of neurons signals the presence of a particular visual feature, then who, or what, reads that message? How, in other words, does the registering and detection of a feature lead to *cognition*? The image of an observing homunculus, so studiously avoided because of its hopeless naiveté, seems to insinuate itself stubbornly into any thoughts on perception.

What is it about the feature extractors that makes them intelligent? It would seem to require an intelligence that gathers all the signaled features into a cognitive whole: a homunculus. We are reminded also of a principle in physics we discussed in chapter 1: *local causality*. How is it possible, we may ask, to connect the different bits of information appearing at the various feature extractors without physical links to all of them? If information processing merely extracts the features *woman*, *red dress*, and *moving*, and stores them in different locations in the brain, it would take a metaphysical entity, a *ghost in the machine*, to reconstruct the original scene.

Alternatively, if these various pieces of information were brought together at a single point, a neuron, this would have to be a wise neuron, a gnostic neuron. We have difficulty ascribing such understanding to a single cell that is buried deep in neural tissue and whose only contacts with the outside world have been occasional bundles of transmitter molecules impinging on its dendrites.

Any theory of perception will have to face another difficulty. Why do different activities in the brain produce different sensations? How do we connect neural activity of a highly coded nature with the real scene we are observing? Why does activity in one part of the brain give us the sensation of looking at a tree, another of watching a ballgame, and yet another of hearing traffic noises? It is as though particular neurons carried labels: "*When lit, you are looking at such-and-such.*" But who makes the labels and who reads them? The concept of *labeled lines* that physiologists often speak of, instead of rescuing us from a dilemma, only leads us farther into the jungle where the homunculus lurks.

As an alternative, we could pin our hopes on processes that occur still farther up in the nervous system, perhaps in the frontal lobes of the cortex where everything may still come together. But we cannot escape the fundamental conundrum that either single neurons are capable of knowing and understanding or else some strange *nonlocal* processes are going on.

The idea of independent and scattered homunculi, each concerned with one of Dennett's multiple drafts, is therefore appealing. Perhaps no convergence is necessary. The illusion given by the illustration below provides an argument against that. What we see there are either two heads facing each other or one vase. Perhaps, somewhere in your cortex, there is a face draft and a vase draft. But as you contemplate the picture, you find that the two interpretations never coexist. Instead, your perception switches back and forth from one to the other. You can always tell which is your current perception. It is as though there were a higher-order homunculus, a *honcho-homunculus*, switching his attention between the face and the vase drafts.

Two drafts—*but you are conscious of only one at a time.*

. . .and Down

I have given a brief account of the traditional view of sensory information processing in the brain and some of the philosophical questions it raises. According to this view the sensory messages travel through the nervous system much like sardines through a cannery or pigs through a slaughterhouse. The key word here is *processing.* I will call this the *slaughterhouse paradigm* of perception. It describes how the initially live image is taken apart and cleaned up in the early stages of processing, its useful features extracted, packaged, labeled, and sent off in different directions.

This view of perception is not wrong, just woefully incomplete. It is based on less than half of what neuroanatomists have been telling us about sensory pathways for almost a century. It was the father of modern neuroanatomy, Santiago Ramón y Cajal, who discovered long ago that alongside the sensory fibers that lead *upward* along the sensory pathway, there are axon bundles that come *down* from the higher brain centers and go back to more peripheral sensory structures. (These returning fiber bundles are not to be confused with the descending pathways that lead from the cortex to the muscles.) Most physiologists, not knowing what to do with these "wrong-way" fibers, have studiously ignored them. But they are there, broad highways of neural traffic coming down from the cortex to the place where the visual messages first enter the brain: the LGN.

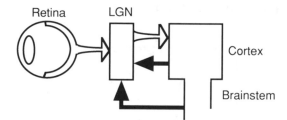

The visual pathway, showing neural fiber bundles returning to the LGN from the cerebral cortex and the brain stem (black arrows).

In the diagram above, we take a second look at this part of the visual pathway. It is still very schematic but now shows the bundle of nerve fibers, several millions of them, that *descends* from the cortex and reenters the LGN. Another bundle is sent back to the LGN from one of the oldest brain structures, the *brain stem.* These wrong-way fibers are indicated by black arrows in the diagram.

Since the only output of the LGN is the one that carries the visual messages to the cortex, we must assume that the function of the fibers returning to the LGN is to modify the sensory messages in some way. This follows again from the principle that there are no terminal neurons. The inescapable conclusion we must draw from the extremely well established anatomical fact of the feedback pathways is that the LGN is not the simple relay we've been told it is, but it participates *actively* in the perceptual process. But unlike the "early processing" that has taken place in the retina, the modifications carried out at the LGN are *at the behest* of higher brain centers, and are therefore expected to inject into the sensory messages information not contained in the primary images received from the retina.

The brain stem sits, as the name implies, at the base of the brain and is one of the oldest structures. It has functions that are both primitive and exalted. A part of it called the brain-stem *reticular formation* has long been known to be essential in the maintenance of consciousness and thought. It is in intimate two-way contact with the cortex, and when it is damaged, or its link to the cortex is interrupted due to disease or injury, the patient lapses into a coma.

The reticular formation is informed of sensory and cognitive events occurring in the cortex. Richard Restak,[5] a neurologist at Georgetown University School of Medicine, reports that "if you think about an ice cream sandwich right now, the idea of it—primarily a product of your cerebral cortex, . . .will stimulate a wave of excitability which will descend into the reticular formation. . . ."

In a sense, the reticular formation in the brain stem not only "knows" what comes in through the senses, but gets an integrated view of what goes on in the cortex. Again, as expressed repeatedly,

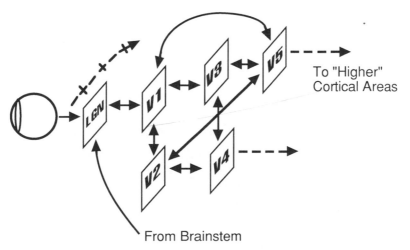

Higher and higher. The visual pathway from eye to cortex.
(For the meaning of the branch labeled + – + – see page 137.)

"knowing" here means nothing other than receiving the information and being able to pass it on.

In the diagram I show in more detail the part of the visual pathway that leads from the eye via the LGN into the cortex. The visual areas in the cortex are labeled V1 through V5, beyond which are regions in the *temporal* (side of the head) and *parietal* (top of the head) parts of the cortex. Note that from the LGN onward all connections are reciprocal, that is, they form *loops*. We simply should not think of the visual pathway as performing one-way, sequential processing on the sense data. The multiple feedback loops increase immensely the complexity of the dynamics taking place here. Is there any way we can understand their function?

There have been a number of speculations concerning these multiple loops, and especially the function of the LGN and the role of the pathways returning to the LGN from the cortex and the brain stem. It is clear that they must somehow alter the transmission characteristics of the LGN. This is sometimes called *filtering*. It is as though the world were viewed through glasses that color or obscure part of reality. But there is no agreement regarding the purpose of these alterations or the mechanisms by which they are accomplished.

Chapter 8

Perception, Imagery, and Creativity

Perception

Where does vision differ from the data acquisition systems—the photographic camera, the video recorder—we mentioned at the beginning of chapter 6? I submit that the neural computer at the end of our visual pathway is only part of the story. The other part has to do with the feedback pathways mentioned in the last chapter. These feedback loops make our sensory systems *self-referent*, and that opens up dynamic possibilities that just could not exist without them. Coupled with a hierarchy of feature extractors and a rich network of associative connections between them, I want to show in this chapter how the transformation of the raw sense data by the fibers coming down from above may make the difference between simple data acquisition and perception. The discussion here will be descriptive; a more detailed dynamic theory is presented in the next chapter and in the appendix.[1]

❦❦❦❦

In engineering language, we distinguish between positive and negative feedback. The latter is a regulating or limiting mechanism. A thermostat is an example of negative feedback: if the temperature is too high, the source of heat is shut off; if the temperature is too low, the source of heat is turned on. Negative feedback establishes conditions of predictability and stability. In positive feedback, by contrast, chance fluctuations are enhanced, instabilities exaggerated, often with explosive consequences. There is a creative element in positive feedback leading often to unpredictable behavior.

I envision the mechanism involved in the control of the LGN to act like a *positive* feedback. Suppose you are looking for a coin you dropped on a beach. Assume that, to aid you in the search, the cortex instructs the LGN to suppress the images of pebbles, leaves, shells, and so on, and to enhance anything small, round, flat, and metallic, in short, anything that looks like a coin. In this selective positive feedback, a mere suggestion of a coin would be made to look even more coinlike to call attention to itself, until closer scrutiny reveals that the search has been successful or that what you were looking at was not a coin after all. Reality will win out in the end because of the persuasiveness of our senses.

Take another example. You are looking at a cloud pattern that vaguely resembles the shape of a rabbit. Somewhere in the cortex, feature analyzers are triggered, and the idea of a rabbit comes to mind. This is signaled back to the LGN, where the cloud pattern is made to look even more suggestive of a rabbit. The feedback mechanism thus pulls a rabbit out of the LGN.

Usually this process cannot continue indefinitely. The cloud is still perceived as a cloud and will not assume a perfect rabbit shape. We may think of what goes on in the LGN as a *competition* between the *reality* that is conveyed from the eyes and the *fancy* that comes down from the cortex. In the normal, alert brain, reality will have a powerful restraining influence on the fancy. We don't often hallucinate. But the image perceived is not the same as the image received, and in the theory cited here, the changes occur not just at the highest levels of cognition but are projected to the periphery of the sensory system.

The dismal scene depicted here is entitled *St. Helena*. We see several trees, a dead stump, and an undefined rectangular slab, looking out over a dreary seascape with what looks like a sailboat in the distance. We are told that Napoleon is somewhere in the picture. But where? Is he buried under the slab? Is he escaping on the sailboat?

I was unable to find him until he was pointed out to me. (I reveal the answer in the endnotes,[2] to give you a chance to test your imagination.) You will find, as I did, that—once you know the answer—you will never again look at the picture without immediately *seeing* Napoleon.

An example in which the received visual pattern was drastically revised by the brain is shown in the next picture. This is a map of the surface of the planet Mars drawn by the American

St. Helena.

astronomer Percival Lowell (1855–1916). Lowell, following suggestions that extensive canal systems had been sighted on Mars, became convinced that intelligent beings had built these irrigation
canals. This conviction caused him to "see" these objects with sufficient clarity to publish a series of maps. We know now, from
detailed satellite surveys of the planet, that most of the features
drawn here—and given names by the author—existed only in
Lowell's imagination.

The process of feature manipulation is normally limited, as
I have stressed, by the persuasive strength of the primary sensory
image. Hallucinatory experiences represent extreme forms of this
process in that images of a pseudo-reality are created. This happens especially in cases of experimental sensory deprivation and
also, of course, in dreaming. What these cases have in common
is that no *real* sensory images from the retina are there to interfere
with the patterns generated by the positive feedback from above,
which thus is free to generate full-blown patterns that can mimic
sensory input. Just like the mapmakers in the days of Columbus,
the brain places the monsters where the map is otherwise blank.

But subtle changes are often discernible in the picture. Look
again at *St. Helena* on this page. If you have already located

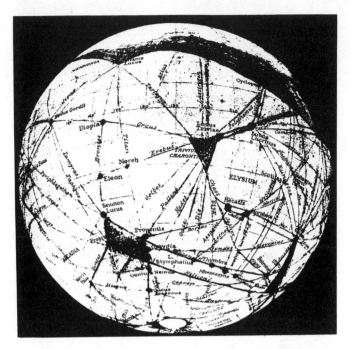

Canals on Mars as drawn by Percival Lowell.

Napoleon, you will find that he now dominates the picture. Every-thing else has become *background*. The area between the two trees now looks brighter, the outlines sharper than anywhere else in the picture.

The Internal Sketchpad and the Creative Loop

The emerging picture of perception thus differs markedly from the model of unidirectional sensory processing (or mere *sensing*) that I have called the *slaughterhouse paradigm*. In perception the sensory message is supplemented with stored information and logical algorithms that can operate retroactively on the incoming sensory data. I will return to this point in chapter 13 in connection with the problem of consciousness.

It turns out that the existence of neural feedback loops is the rule rather than the exception for connectivity in the nervous sys-tem: If a region *A* in the brain sends many fibers to another region, *B*, it is highly likely that *B* also sends fibers back to *A*. The brain is full of such loops (see illustration on page 65). Thus the kind of process that I have proposed for the LGN, and which I call the *creative loop*, also may take place at other levels along the visual and other sensory pathways.

Positive feedback loops, as we stated before, constitute inherently unstable mechanisms. Particular fluctuations are amplified selectively so that features not initially present at the input may be *generated* in a *bootstrap* fashion. I think of the LGN not as a simple *relay* between retina and cortex, but as a *sketchpad* on which the cortex expresses its fancy by drawing and erasing.

We must assume for our model that fluctuations, or *noise*, exist somewhere in the system to be selected and amplified. But what determines the fluctuations selected for amplification and the mechanisms by which these processes are carried out? How does the LGN *know* what features are "fancied" by the cortex? We will come back to these questions in the next chapter and in the appendix.

The modifications are generally such that they don't conflict with obvious features in the primary visual pattern. If they are grossly at variance with reality, we speak of hallucinations. Hallucinatory patterns are readily created when visual input is absent, such as in cases of sensory deprivation or in sleep. Out of shimmering noise and fleeting fragments that populate the higher centers, the brain somehow sketches the shapes that appear in our dreams.

Dreaming occurs during phases of sleep called REM (for *rapid eye movement*, which is the distinctive feature of this phase). REM sleep has been studied extensively by the Harvard psychiatrist J. A. Hobson,[3] who found that particular centers in the brain stem are responsible for switching the brain from ordinary sleep to REM sleep and back again. The same switching affects the feedback pathways through which the brain stem exerts strong influence on the LGN.

If this idea of a creative loop formed by the reentering pathways is correct, it could contribute to our understanding of so-called cognitive processes. We have replaced the picture of sequential processing of sensory information, the slaughterhouse paradigm, which always brought up the nagging question of who, or what, ultimately looked at the processed and labeled neural signals. Instead, we now can view perception as a unitary process, in which central and peripheral areas of the brain cooperate in a bootstrap fashion. The neural message does not have to be read by any homunculus. It reads itself.

The need for something like the creative loop was oddly anticipated by the Renaissance monk Gregor Reisch, whose sketch of the brain appears on page 40. If we look carefully at the first chamber, the *sensus communis* that gathers all the raw sense data, we see there the words *fantasia* and *imaginativa*, clearly suggesting that the sensory messages are modified by fantasy and imagination before being passed on to the next level.

We may look on the creative loop also as a particular example of that old philosophical conundrum called *self-reference*. A statement, or proposition, is self-referent if part of it contains a statement about itself. This often leads to seemingly unresolvable paradoxes. The assertion "What I am saying now is a lie" is a classic example. If the statement is true—that is, *not* a lie—then it *is* a lie. But that makes the statement true again. There is no way out of the trap.

Not all self-referent assertions are paradoxical. There is, however, often something elusive, almost mysterious, in self-reference. It has the potential to create something out of nothing. We call this a *bootstrap* process: A germ of an idea is projected into the picture, like Reisch's *fantasia* and *imaginativa* (page 40), and reinforces itself by being cycled through the loop. Lowell's suspicion that there might be canals on Mars makes canals.

The model of perception I have proposed here is reminiscent of the concept of *projection* that used to be popular among psychologists. It was argued that the information received and perceived at the highest levels of the brain must be somehow bounced back, or *projected* into the outside world, because that is where we perceive the event to be taking place. I see and hear you talking *out there*, not in my visual or auditory cortex.

This somewhat fuzzy argument is derided by Dennett[4] as a revival of the *Cartesian Theater*. In defense of this he also cites a well-known statement by Bertrand Russell:[5]

> *Whoever accepts the causal theory of perception is compelled to conclude that percepts are in our heads, for they come at the end of a causal chain of physical events leading, spatially, from the object to the brain of the percipient. We cannot suppose that, at the end of this process, the last effect suddenly jumps back to the starting point like a stretched rope when it snaps.*

These criticisms unfairly dismiss the idea of projection as metaphysical, simply because no physical basis was envisioned. In the slaughterhouse paradigm of sensory processing, a sausage will never again become a pig. Real sensory pathways, however, are not one-way *causal chains* but elaborate systems of loops that allow the highest cortical levels to reach back toward the world of objects.

Imagery and Creativity

"Thinking," says the Harvard psychologist Stephen Kosslyn, "is the ability to contemplate something in its absence."[6] Thinking thus requires imagery, a phenomenon closely linked to perception for which I presented a neural model above. There is a history of controversy over the nature of mental images and their location in the brain. A common view is that, because imagery is an advanced function of the mind, it must reside at the highest levels of the human brain, certainly in the cerebral cortex, perhaps in the frontal lobe of the cortex. It would seem a reasonable extension of this view to say that such images consist of symbolic, coded, perhaps verbal, representations, characteristic of these levels.

However, many psychologists now believe that the mental image of a rose or of a rabbit is *eidetic*, that it has the spatial qualities of a picture rather than being more like an idea, or a symbol, expressed at high levels by a neural code. But the pictorial neural representations occur near the beginning of the sensory pathways, not at the ends.

Evidence for an eidetic, picturelike character of mental images comes from many experiments carried out by psychologists over the past two decades. In one of these,[7] subjects were asked to match pairs of simple geometrical figures, where one figure was rotated with respect to the other. The authors report that the time required for matching depended on the angle through which one figure had to be rotated to coincide with the other. For a large disparity, the subjects required a longer time. This was interpreted to indicate that the subjects performed a *mental* rotation of images that had spatial properties similar to those of the objects.

Other experiments carried out by Kosslyn and his collaborators, measured the times required to scan a mental image, such as a map, and again found that these scanning times increased in proportion with the distances on the map.[8]

It must be admitted that none of these experiments unequivocally excludes what has been called a propositional vs. an eidetic representation of mental images, although they are strongly suggestive of the second. Rotating the coded symbol of an object does not produce the same effect as rotating the object. But there are difficulties with this interpretation. Kosslyn, who is one of the chief proponents of the theory of eidetic representation, is doubtful about a *literal* interpretation of mental images as *pictures*. A "literal picture in the head," Kosslyn states, "would require some way in which we could look at it." But, he asserts, "no examination of the brain has turned up either a screen or an eye to watch it."

I here propose the literal interpretation of the mental picture hypothesis. A screen, I believe, *does* exist, probably a series of screens, the lowest and most pictorial being the LGN. (The human retina is probably not accessible to feedback from above, although there are some claims that it is.) If the mental act requires detailed spatial examination, a picturelike image will be projected onto the "screen" of the LGN. The necessary neural pathways exist, and in the next chapter I will propose a specific and plausible mechanism for this process. No special *inner eye* would be required, because the information would be conveyed to the brain, just as if it were that of a real image picked up by the eyes.

I mentioned that similar feedback processes may occur at different levels along the sensory pathway. I would assume that the nature of a mental image and its location would depend on the requirements of the cognitive act it subserves. Thus, if I ask you "What is your grandmother's first name?" your answer requires only a manipulation of verbal symbols. But if I say "Don't you think your grandmother looks like Golda Meir?" the relationships between symbols and propositions, stored at higher brain centers, will be of little help. You will need more of a pictorial representation to decide the answer.

If "thinking is the ability to contemplate something in its absence," in Kosslyn's words, then *creativity* is the ability to contemplate something that has never existed before. This applies to the artist who creates new visions, the writer, the composer, the scientist who conceives of a new theory, the mathematician, the architect, the inventor—in short, anyone who goes beyond the routine in his or her profession. We value creativity as one of the most significant achievements of the human brain. Can we say anything about possible mechanisms?

Again, we are tempted to look for this function at the highest cortical levels. But it is instructive to examine the procedure employed in some of these creative acts. An artist may have an idea for a painting, but he may not immediately go to the canvas. Instead, he often begins with a series of sketches.

But why sketch? Why is it necessary to *externalize* the idea conceived in the brain, and then have the brain examine it? For a composer, the keyboard serves as the sketchpad. In every creative act we observe this bootstrap process in which nascent ideas are externalized and then taken in again by the brain to be reexamined and modified in a *creative loop*.

But sketchpads and keyboards are relatively recent acquisitions to aid our creative activities. If the picture I have drawn of the seeing and perceiving brain is correct, then similar processes are built into our brains. There are internal sketchpads—the LGN is one—on which higher brain centers can project their creative ideas by top-down control, so they can be contemplated, judged, and perfected. The internal sketchpad is the peripheral end of a creative loop. It must have played an essential role in the earliest acts of human creative animation, the fashioning of the primitive tools that started us on the road to civilization.

Humans are not the only beings that possess the neural feedback circuitry that I interpreted as forming a creative loop. The LGN with its massive feedback from above is a mammalian characteristic, and probably serves similar purposes in most mammals. The use of tools by some primates is well documented, but the tools come ready made, like the sticks chimpanzees use to extract termites from their mounds. There is very little, if any, tool*making* by nonhumans. The creative loop is there, but it functions at a much more restricted level.

The internal sketchpad has its limitations, however, even in the human brain. The images drawn on it are ghostly and evanescent. It is difficult to hold complex patterns in our mind for long and subject them to detailed scrutiny. This must have been a severe limitation to our earliest creative drives. We can now appreciate the enormous advantage humans gained when they invented (or discovered) the ability to *complete the projection*, that is, to externalize their mental images beyond the sketchpad of the LGN by creating permanent images in the world around them.

We don't know when and how this ability to create external images originated. It is unique to the human animal and as essential a step toward future progress as making tools or the invention of language. The period of the paleolithic wall paintings and carvings that fill many of the caves in southern France and Spain was called a *creative explosion*. We are awed by the color and movement in the silent procession of prehistoric beasts across the big wall of the famous cave of Lascaux—bison, bulls, rhino, ibex, wild horses, a herd of deer fording a stream—all drawn with the gravity of illustrations for a children's fairy tale.

Much has been written about the supposed purpose of these efforts. Were they the basis of unknown rites or celebrations? Were they religious? But perhaps these prehistoric humans painted for the sheer joy of exercising this newfound talent. And perhaps the earliest of these artistic expressions were not even meant to be seen by other humans. This is suggested by the inaccessibility of many of these works. John E. Pfeiffer, in his book *Creative Explosion*, describes how, in the Nerja Cave in southern Spain, one has to climb a forty-five foot wall, then maneuver precariously around a huge stalagmite, turn on one's back in a tight recess, to be suddenly confronted with the images of a long-necked hind, an ibex, and a fish.[9]

But if these images were not meant for an audience, they were only the artist's communication with himself, a soliloquy through which to test and expand his own sense of color, form, and movement, and knowledge of detail about the world.

PART THREE

IMAGE AND REALITY

*The image precedes the reality
it is supposed to represent.*

R. Kearney, *The Wake of Imagination*

✸✸✸✸

*It started simply enough:
just a pulse in the lowest registers—bassoons and
bassett horns—like a rusty squeezebox. It would
have been comic except for the slowness, which
gave it instead a sort of serenity. And then suddenly, high above it, sounded a single note on the
oboe. It hung there unwavering—piercing me
through—till breath could hold it no longer, and
a clarinet withdrew it out of me, and sweetened
it into a phrase of such delight, it had me
trembling.*

(Antonio Salieri, on hearing Mozart's Serenade
for Thirteen Wind Instruments.)
From *Amadeus*, Peter Shaffer

Chapter 9

Images of Reality—
Reality of Images

Images are facsimiles, incomplete and fanciful copies of reality that we fashion with our hands for our eyes to look at. We also speak of *mental images*, visual apparitions that exist in our heads only and are generally not open to scrutiny by others. We ourselves are uncertain about their true character, their location and origin in the brain, and their function. But there appears to be, in the words of the psychologists Lynn Cooper and Roger Shepard,[1] a ''demonstrable correspondence between mental imagery and its physical analogues.'' Whether this correspondence amounts to a true pictorial or *iconic* reproduction of reality in the brain, or a symbolic or *coded* representation, is a matter of dispute.[2]

In the primitive classical view, the brain elaborates images of reality and presents them for inspection to a nonphysical intelligence, a spirit, a wise homunculus who freely bases his/her/its decisions on the material revealed as *pictures-in-the-head*. The images play as on a stage, which the philosopher Dennett calls the *Cartesian Theater*. This stage/mind duality has fallen into disrepute among most of today's neuroscientists, and with it the idea of mental images that have anything like a true pictorial character. But, although it is appropriate to dispose of that pesky homunculus that explains nothing, I question the hasty dismissal of the picture-in-the-head. We shall see, incidentally, that, instead of disappearing, the homunculus has been merely fragmented in some of the current theories that set out to avoid all nonphysical processes and explain all mental phenomena through strictly physical mechanisms.

We will in the next chapter take up some of the available mechanisms and the requirements they will have to fulfill. But first, a look at the images.

Perhaps we can learn to understand images in the head if we look first at the properties and function of the images we make in the external world. The paintings, sculptures, icons, hold for us a special kind of mystery and fascination. We have learned, somehow, to *see* things in them that aren't there, to conjure up under their influence, a pseudo-reality that may be evocative and yet subtly, or magically, or radically, different from the real thing.

Paris street scenes, as they appear in early daguerreotypes, have an unreal quality about them. There are no people. Did the photographer wait until everybody was out of the way? Did he or she snap the picture at dawn before anyone was up?

The answer is that these early examples of photography required exposure times of many minutes, during which people will have come and gone, leaving not even a streak in the picture. What remained was only the solid, immobile part of the city. And since the picture itself became a bit of frozen reality, it probably did not strike these early photographers as strange that only the permanent was imaged. Perhaps they would have found a modern photograph of a street scene unreal, with all the people frozen in mid-stride and a child playing hopscotch miraculously suspended in midair, never to touch ground again.

Realism of an image thus appears to be a matter of convention. The story is told about a man who approached Picasso after seeing his *Demoiselles d'Avignon* and asked the artist why he didn't paint people the way they really looked. "Well, how do they really look?" asked Picasso. The man then took a photograph of his wife from his wallet. "Like this," he said. Picasso looked at the picture; then, handing it back, he said, "She is small, isn't she. And flat."

Time and space are the rigid framework, the stage on which the world of objects displays its events. Modern physics has forced us to reexamine and redefine these old concepts, but without some firm notions of time and space we could not come to any understanding of nature and its laws.

The two examples of early daguerreotypes and Picasso's painting illustrate some of the subtle changes of the meanings of time and space in the process of creating images.

Often we do not realize just how much our brain has to add to a picture to make it a recognizable scene. The canvas by the American painter Mark Tansey, entitled *The Innocent Eye Test*, depicts a cow being shown a life-size painting of cows. A group of scientists is standing by with clipboards at the ready to record the cow's reaction. There doesn't seem to be any. The cow could be looking at a fencepost.

The Innocent Eye Test, *by Mark Tansey (by permission of the Metropolitan Museum of Art, New York).*

The painting—the one that is hanging in the Metropolitan Museum of Art in New York—and the painting within the painting are both monochrome, the color of old sepia photographs. This is to emphasize, no doubt, the fact that the real cow, the one being shown the image, is itself a painting, as flat and lifeless as the others. They are all painted, same size, same style, but we see one as a cow, the others as a painting of cows. The first cow is unimpressed. It can't paint, therefore it can't understand the painting.

The Picture-in-the-Head

But what about *mental* images? I argued in chapter 8 that the feedback pathway could perhaps generate pictorial representations at the various "screens" that form the visual pathway. What are the functions of these images, and what could be their neurological bases? And what about the objections to the picture-in-the-head?

Let us dispose of the *guilt-by-association* that has been a chief argument against this concept: the fact that it has been a major ingredient in the classical dualism that envisions scenes played on the Cartesian stage and viewed by a homunculus. It may be objected that without the homunculus there doesn't seem to be much need for the picture. But there is nothing mysterious or non-physical about a neural activity mimicking the activity that would be produced by sensory stimulation.

Both Kosslyn[3] and Dennett[4] argue against the existence of *real* mental images, pointing out that there is no inner screen for them to be displayed, no inner eye to look at them, and, anyway, no light in the head for them to be seen. These arguments are, I believe, specious.

The retinal image itself, although the only thing in the visual pathway that is made of light, tells us nothing. Neither does its translation into the electrochemical outputs of the rods and cones, or the pattern of activity of the retinal ganglion cells, or similar activity in the LGN. There is a lot more to perception. We saw that the visual pathway consists of a sequence of *sheets* of neurons, each of which is a kind of screen, and any activity produced along the way is *seen* by stations higher up. Thus stimulation of the optic nerve by electrical or mechanical means will be perceived by the system as flashes of light. No one is naive enough to suggest that these or the activity patterns of mental images—if they exist— require light in order to be seen. This should dispose of the argument that there is no eye to look at the images and no light for them to be seen.

There is, however, a more serious question about mental images that are true pictures-in-the-head, being produced through top-down control at centers as peripheral as the LGN. This problem was raised years ago by the neurophysiologist Karl Pribram, who was trying to interpret the function of the massive neural pathways that lead from higher visual centers in the cortex back to the LGN in the thalamus.[5] These wrong-way fibers evidently affect the sensory pattern that the LGN relays to the cortex. But if these modifications are to be specific for particular input patterns, how can we expect the relatively primitive LGN, following simple commands coming down from the cortex, to make a cloud pattern more rabbitlike, let alone paint a pinto horse there when we hallucinate or dream? If we take the picture-in-the-head concept seriously, something like this must happen, if not at the LGN then at one of the next levels of visual processing where the sensory messages still have a somewhat picturelike character.

The difficulty with all this is what is sometimes called the *problem of the inverse*. If the visual pathway consists of a sequence of stations that extract different features from the original scene, generating responses that are progressively more coded, that is, unlike the original picture, it is not clear how this process can be reversed. It is like expecting that by triggering the alarm of a smoke detector by some other means, smoke would be produced at the other end. How, in other words, can the thought of a horse produce the image of a horse?

Indeed, the conceptual difficulty of feature generation as the *inverse* of feature detection has led the noted neurophysiologist and Nobel laureate Sir John Eccles to proclaim that "at no stage in the nervous processing can neurons be found that would be instrumental in the eventual reconstruction of the picture."[6] But the feedback pathways from V1 to LGN evidently do *something*. I have proposed that the LGN is used by the cortex as a kind of sketchpad on which just such a reconstruction is carried out.

Alopex: A Mechanism for Pattern Generation

There have been suggestions that the feedback pathways somehow modify and filter the incoming sensory messages.[7] I proposed in 1976 a more drastic role for the LGN: it not only filters but also supplements and *creates* input patterns under the guidance of cortical feedback.[8] The necessary *inversion* of the sensory process could be accomplished by an optimization process (see appendix). I suggested a particular algorithm I called *Alopex*, and later showed that very simple neural circuitry of the type encountered in the LGN could account for the process.[9] More recently, David Mumford, a biomathematician at Harvard University, proposed a very similar role for the V1-LGN loop, without, however, presenting a specific neural mechanism.[10]

Alopex is an evolutionary process in which peripheral patterns evolve toward a fittest pattern, that is, one causing the strongest central response. The idea is that the feedback pathways to the LGN inform the LGN of the strength of the response to what is being relayed to the cortex by the LGN. (If this statement sounds confusing, it only reflects the complexity caused by the self-referent character of this loop.) The LGN, in turn, is wired in such a way that it modifies its own activity pattern so as to maximize the strength of the feedback signal. A brief explanation of the algorithm carried out by the Alopex process is given in the appendix.

The process requires the presence of some random events, or *noise*, to be added to the picture. There are several possible sources for this. Neurons have been observed to fire spontaneously, for no apparent reason. Thus, in the absence of visual scenes received from the eye, the sheets of neurons in the LGN may look like the random sparkle of a lake on a windy day. This random flickering is transmitted to the cortex, where feature analyzers and interpreters go to work on the cryptic messages. Is there a face, an animal? It is like looking at an inkblot or a cloud pattern, with one exception: The brain can reach out and *manipulate* the pattern. If it does this in a way that enhances the cortical sensation, then it might create images even though nothing is received from the eyes. All it needs is some noise, some random sparkle on which to build.

As an example of the process proposed here, if the idea of a horse, originating somewhere in the cortex, is projected back to the LGN by this process, horselike neural activity patterns will arise there. These, in turn, will be seen by higher sensory centers and strengthen the central thought about a horse. The loop is completed. If this happens while you are in REM sleep, the horse may come complete with pinto spots and prance convincingly across your field of view.

There has been much discussion over the presence of noise in the nervous system. For a long time, physiologists have shied away from the notion that anything random is going on in the brain. But noise need not be totally capricious and unrelated to the serious business of dealing with the world outside. Consider the fact that, in your lifetime, your nervous system has taken in a seemingly endless procession of images—some fleeting and irrelevant, some strongly linked to others, and of lasting significance. We are able to recall many of them in detail; some turn up unexpectedly, recalled by new events, and become effective in determining our behavior. Some influence our actions without entering our awareness.

Our brain seems to be constantly occupied with something, a task at hand, or idle ruminations, when left to itself. The paths taken in such undirected thinking may be influenced by what our senses bring in at the time, or, as portrayed by Rodin's *Thinker*, may be free-running. In the latter case, it will be old events, stored as memories and memorized associations and rules, that pilot our thoughts. But the itinerary is difficult to trace. More often than not, we are unaware of what made us think of a particular thing. It seems reasonable to suppose that a whole spectrum of influences exists, some strong and easily recognized, others so faint that they are untraceable.[11] It is that multitude of minute specks in your memory, the dust left behind from a million unremarkable past events, that must form a background noise in your brain and may determine at this moment what you are thinking.

We have tested this idea of pattern generation through feedback pathways by simulating on a computer a neural net that has the following properties. When this net (box B in diagram) is shown a pattern by a device A, it will return a response to A. This response R is a composite of responses of pattern recognition devices built into B. Each of these is designed to detect a particular face.

In our experiment, B contained four such face detectors, one of which was a digitized photograph of Einstein. The box A, which is a subroutine in the computer program, carries out the Alopex algorithm described in the appendix; it will modify the pattern it sends to B in a way that will increase R.

It must be emphasized that there is nothing in A that knows anything about faces, and that R can tell A only whether its pattern has become *better* or *worse*.

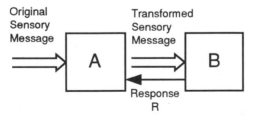

Modification of a sensory input pattern. A sensory relay station, A, is transmitting a pattern to B and modifies it according to the response R received from B.

The experimental arrangement shown in the above figure should be compared with the schematic diagram of the visual pathway on page 64. Here, box *A* is analogous to the LGN, and *B* to the higher centers, including cortex and brain stem.

The Alopex algorithm is somewhat like the game we have all played as children, in which a person is to find an object others have hidden in a room. He or she is at first walking about randomly and then told whether he or she is getting closer ("you are getting warmer") or going away ("you are getting colder") from the object. Alopex is a game like this, played not in three dimensions but in thousands.

In one experiment, *A* receives a "sensory input" obtained by superimposing noise on a picture of Einstein (see *a* below). When the loop is activated, this pattern changes gradually until the resemblance to Einstein is no longer in doubt. The only thing that guided the process is the feedback response telling *A* whether it is getting warmer or colder. Meanwhile the brightness at each picture element fluctuates randomly, but is gradually pushed by the Alopex algorithm to assume its appropriate value in the picture.

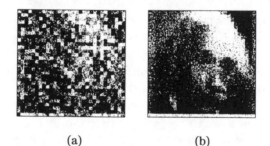

(a)   (b)

Computer simulation of pattern modification by feedback:
(a) *sensory input;* (b) *modified pattern.*

In other experiments, we wanted to see what would happen when there was no "sensory input" pattern. When the process was started with a blank "screen" at *A*, the noise added would always converge to form *one* of the faces to which *B* is sensitive, but never a combination of them. Which face appears is not predictable, because the process depends on random contributions. The function of *A* is thus to select a single pattern from the various possibilities offered by *B*.

The upshot of this somewhat technical discussion can now be simply stated: An intermediate station in the visual path, the LGN, for example, acts as a screen, or stage, or sketchpad, on which incoming patterns are modified before being passed on. Patterns also can be *invented* there, especially when no sensory input exists. These processes are governed by optimization algorithms for which Alopex is a plausible candidate. Moreover, the self-referent loop also provides the *selective property* that allows for self-enhancement of only a single item at a time.

The Cartesian stage is not such a bad metaphor after all. In the picture I have drawn we find sensory messages enacted at peripheral neural projection areas such as the LGN. When nothing real is happening—when we dream or daydream—these same stages become like marionette theaters, with the higher levels of the cerebral cortex being both audience and puppeteer.

Unreal Images

When fancy is not held in check by the reports from the senses, some "internal logician" generally will see to it that the imaged and imagined are not wildly at odds with the rules of logic and the laws of the world of objects. This censorship is somewhat relaxed in dreams, where all sorts of irrational and unrealistic scenarios can be played out.

But even our waking images and thoughts are often tinged with unreality. Illusions and delusions are commonplace. What is perceived is different from what is reported by the senses, and what is remembered is different from what is perceived. We fantasize and we confabulate. There is in all of us what I would call a *facto-fugal* streak, which makes me wonder whether this may not have evolved as an adaptive advantage. We gravitate toward the fantastic. Against the ponderous fact of our earthbound bodies, a few humans have kept alive the vision that man can fly. Humans don't always accept the seemingly irrational as impossible. To be *visionary* is to see what others can't yet see, and civilization could not have advanced to its present state without the willingness of some to pursue stubbornly what others see only as a will-o'-the-wisp.

Although we could not do without the occasional success of the visionary, we cannot condone everything that defies reason. The discovery of a live coelacanth, believed to have been extinct for millions of years, is no argument for the existence of sea monsters, Bigfoot, or the Abominable Snowman. It is necessary to fight the monsters so that only overwhelming evidence will allow one occasionally to slip through our rational defenses. We find a parallel of sorts in the effects of radiation. Weak background radiation is largely responsible for naturally occurring mutations and for evolution. Without this radiation we could not have evolved to our present biological state. But radiation is also harmful, because—apart from damaging the individual—most mutations are detrimental. Hence, nobody in his right mind would purposely increase the radiation level, arguing that it might improve our species.

Neither should we accept propositions we find laughable just because some great ideas were once laughed at. This may seem unfair to the unrecognized genius, but we simply cannot build a structure of knowledge if we accept every crackpot idea as a potential gem. Similarly, we must not label as art every pretense at art, just because in the past we failed to recognize some masterpieces.

One other side to our imagings and imaginings is perhaps the hardest to understand. It concerns questions on which neither our senses nor our logic can shed much light: questions of *ultimate purpose*, of universal justice, reward and retribution, and ultimate destiny of individuals or the human race. We have filled in these blank areas with a rich tapestry of myths and belief systems, in defense of which some of us are ready to kill.

Mental imagery is virtually unlimited in its inventiveness. But why have such pictures-in-the-head if there is no Cartesian Theater and no homunculus to watch them? Why couldn't mental imagery take place merely at high cortical levels where only codes and symbols are being manipulated? Many psychologists believe that is exactly what happens. In chapter 11, I will discuss what I think is the role of mental images in the mechanics of thought processes. But first, because I take a *physicalist* approach to mental phenomena, we must take a closer look at the underlying physical system, the *brain*.

Chapter 10

Dynamics of Brain and Mind

Perhaps our brains are time machines—machines that can send and receive messages coming from the past and the future.
Fred Alan Wolf, *Parallel Universes*

We begin with what I consider a safe but not very profound statement about the mind-brain connection: Having a live, functioning brain is a necessary condition for having a thought. Even this minimal assertion is often disputed, which is why I think it is important to state it here, axiomatically, and without further discussion.

Having followed visual information as far as the upper branches of the visual pathway (chapter 7), we are still a long way from understanding thought processes. What happens in the rest of the neural jungle of the cortex?

In the course of the history of brain research, the brain mechanisms proposed to explain mental phenomena have kept pace with the state of physics and technology. Early explanations using hydraulics and clockworks have been replaced by electrochemical mechanisms. To these classical processes we may now have to add such new, esoteric phenomena as chaotic processes, quantum effects, and—in the opinion of one researcher—a not yet discovered *correct quantum gravity*.[1]

A description, however sophisticated, of the world of billions of neurons that send their chemical messages over trillions of synapses still does not tell us what thoughts are crossing our mind. There seem to be two different realms, the one of neurons and their interconnections, studied by physiologists, and the other of emotions, thoughts, and images that are the psychologist's domain. This apparent duality is suggested most strongly by the fact that time and space, which are the touchstones of physical reality, have meanings that are at least different in the world of the mind.

This is not a very happy situation, from the scientist's point of view. We like unification, a common language expressing universal laws. *Reductionism* is a term, often used pejoratively, describing the attempt to express what goes on in the mind in terms of established physical laws. Often this is achieved at the cost of having to deny the existence of some mental phenomena.

Meanwhile, neurophysiology and psychology exist side by side. Are they perhaps just two languages describing the same phenomena?

Time and Space in Brain and Mind

The brain is not just a vast and complex network of cells and fibers. Inscribed in this world are the physical traces left by all of our personal sensory experiences and all the thoughts concerning these experiences that have passed through our mind. The dynamics of this system at any moment are affected by the totality of these experiences. The subtle complexity of this physical system easily transcends any attempt at a detailed description. I want to argue, furthermore, that the description of the dynamics in terms of ordinary time and space—even if it could be achieved—may turn out to be inappropriate.

A single neuron may receive signals from thousands of other neurons, some close by, others a considerable distance away. A neuron A may affect another neuron, B, directly (see diagram), but send its signals to F only via a circuitous path involving three other neurons C, D, and E. Thus, even though F appears closer to A than B, we should call B *closer* because the distance a signal has to travel to go from A to B is shorter than the path from A to F.

But if we make connectivity the criterion of *distance*, then the neural network represents a very strange kind of space. Recall that all connections between neurons are *one-way* paths for signals to travel. This gives rise to another peculiar property. While the distance from A *to* F is long, as we have seen, to go *from F to A* takes only a single short step in this net. Also, while a single step will take you from A to B, there is no way to get back from B to A.

When we talk about *spatial* distribution of neural activity, we are dealing with a space that is quite unlike the one in which we locate the physical objects we are observing.

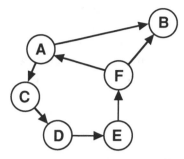

*A hypothetical net of six neurons. Note that all connections between
individual neurons are* one-way, *in striking contrast to connections
between* groups *of neurons, which are often reciprocal.
(See diagram on page 65.)*

You may object that the neural world is, after all, a physical
system, and that ordinary space should be the appropriate description. But the ordinary distances are almost irrelevant, because we
could distort the above diagram of the neural net by stretching
or shortening some of the connections without affecting the functioning of the net. And while it is true that neurons that are close
together in the ordinary sense of the word are also more likely
to be connected, this is by no means a rigid rule.

In the mind, space has even less meaning than in the world
of neurons. In the mental landscape, all things are equally accessible as on a picture postcard. The foreground tree is as near as the
mountains or the clouds. Space is compressed into a flat panorama
with the closest and the remotest event only a thought away.

The role of time in the neural net is equally ambiguous. The
time a neuron fires, which lasts about a thousandth of a second,
can be determined with great precision by means of *microelectrodes*. These are very fine probes that can be inserted directly
into the cell body of a neuron. The technique, which was perfected
in the 1940s, gave neuroscience research a tremendous boost, but
also made neurophysiologists believe that an absolute timescale
can be established for events in the neurocosm.

This is a delusion. When the physiologist monitors two neurons
by means of microelectrodes and finds that their action potentials
reach his instruments at the same time, he says that they fired
simultaneously. But this simultaneity means little inside the neural
net, since the two events may not appear to be simultaneous to
any other neuron in the net. Add to this that signal velocities vary
greatly among different fibers, and that the same signal may arrive

at a given neuron at different times and via different paths, and it will become clear that the role of time in the neurocosm is at least very different from time as we generally conceive of it. Strictly speaking, we cannot think of events in the neurocosm as being arranged along a unique time line, except to that extraneous observer with his microelectrodes. Hence, unless we assume that a *single internal observer* is located somewhere in the brain, the timing of any neural event can be only the time recorded by an external observer.

Therefore, a proper description of the activity of the neural mass would seem to require an external observer who has simultaneous and instantaneous access to all parts of the brain.

Signals picked up by different microelectrodes are easily superimposed on the screen of a cathode ray oscilloscope, and their arrival times determined with great precision. But since no such unique comparisons are possible *within* the neural system, the usual spatio-temporal description of neural activity, so diligently sought by neurophysiologists, is artificial and may not be the ideal framework for describing brain function.

It is easiest to apply our conventional concepts of time and space to the periphery of the neural system, which interacts directly with the world of objects either through sensors or the effectors that control the muscles. In the early stages of vision, as we have pointed out, form and timing are approximately those of the object seen. But the visual image that is gathered by the rods and cones of the retina begins to get scrambled even in the early portions of the visual pathway. There is convergence and divergence among the millions of fibers that convey the message. This means that a single point on the retina affects large areas in subsequent neural mappings. Conversely, any one neuron in, say, the LGN or the visual areas of the cortex is affected not just by one corresponding point on the retina but by sensors spread over large retinal areas.

This fact of spatial scrambling may seem puzzling at first glance, but must be a necessary condition to our perception of form and space. To perceive an object as square or round, we must be able to bring together and compare signals coming from different portions of the object; that is, the neural connectivity must have elements of divergence and convergence. To perceive the shape of an object from the shading of light over its surface, the brightness of one area must be compared with that of another.

But such comparison has as a minimal requirement the superposition of spatial information; that is, it requires *convergence*.

A similar situation exists with respect to time. To perceive motion or any other ongoing change, one also must bring together and compare past and present. Hence, an instantaneous event such as a brief flash of light will be *imaged* in the neural world by activity that may be sustained for several seconds. This has to do in part with the fact that neural pathways are devious, and the speeds with which the signals are propagated vary from less than a foot per second to hundreds of feet per second. The same information thus may arrive at a given place in the brain via different routes and at different times. There also may be reverberations, like multiple echoes between reciprocally connected neural centers. See below a graph of neural activity that was recorded in my laboratory from a part of a frog's brain called the optic tectum in response to a stimulus that was a single brief flash of light.[2] We see that the activity starts about one-tenth of a second after the flash, then rises and falls several times, and ends with a brief burst about six-tenths of a second after the stimulus.

We must conclude from this and many similar experiments that the mapping of visual reality into neural representation is neither point-to-point nor instant-to-instant. And just as a single neuron anywhere in the visual pathway is affected by sensors covering large retinal areas, so the activity at any given moment is determined by visual input stretching back over a broad band of past time.

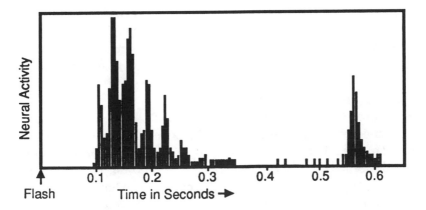

Activity of a neuron in frog tectum following a brief light stimulus.

Without such spatial and temporal mixing we would see discrete image points, rather than *objects*, and a succession of unrelated stills, rather than motion.

In chapter 1, I described the world of objects as "a dissembled world, where each bit of matter follows its own course, isolated from all the others in space and time." With the convergence and divergence of the neural pathways in the peripheral sensory systems, we begin to stitch together a subjective reality that becomes progressively more all-encompassing until past, present, and future are joined in a unit that defines both the unique self and the world around him. More on that later.

Spatial and temporal mixing must occur in other senses as well. Understanding speech or appreciation of music would not be possible without it. It is not the musical note or chord picked up by your ear at this instant that makes it joyful or sad, but the fact that it is embedded in the past and borne by the anticipation of the future.

Consider Salieri's comment, in Peter Shaffer's play *Amadeus*, at the beginning of Part III (page 77). It would not have been a "phrase of such delight" had the sound of the oboe been a thing of the past by the time the sound of the clarinet reached the brain. But it was not the *memory* of the oboe; its sound simply had not yet left the brain but remained as the background on which the sound of the clarinet was superimposed. (It would be just as valid to say that the response to the sound of the oboe is affected by the *future* sound of the clarinet.)

Thus the response (image) of a given event A, formed at a given location in the brain, and hence its sensation, may depend not only on preceding events, but also on events that happen *after* A. A well-known example of this is what psychologists call *backward masking*. In this phenomenon the response to a stimulus may be *masked*—that is, suppressed—when another stimulus of either greater intensity or greater significance follows shortly on the first stimulus.

There are many other examples in which the flow of time that is so unequivocal in the world of objects may be reversed in the world of the mind. In *operant conditioning*, a concept prominent in Skinnerian psychology, reflexes are formed not by the coincidence of two stimuli, as in Pavlov's dog, but by what Skinner[3] has called *selection by consequences*. It means that present behavior—*operant behavior*, as Skinner calls it—is not wholly determined by the past but requires us to peer into the future. Purposive behavior, as I have pointed out before, involves a kind of time reversal in which future events determine the present.

We spoke in the last chapter of a top-down control by which higher brain centers use lower levels as sketchpads or mirrors from which nascent ideas are reflected. In the case of *purposive behavior*, the future—by being mirrored in the brain—acts as the top-down control. The future is, in fact, already present in our mind, and hence in the nervous system, *before* it happens in the world of objects. The tennis player already *knows* the sound and the feel of connecting with the ball while it is still approaching him. Most of the stimuli our senses convey to the brain are already obsolete before they get there. We are aware of the scenery before us and *know* where a moving object is going to be in the next instant. Discrepancies between what we know and what we see either will startle us or will make us suppress what we see. We would *not* do most of the things we do if we didn't already know the outcome. I would not sit at my word processor now punching keys if I didn't know that this would result in magnetic images being put on a disk that could sometime in the near future cause my printer to produce a typescript of what I am thinking now.

Chaos and Determinism

Events in the world of neurons and thoughts are much less predictable than in the world of objects. With time and space having such debatable meanings here, can we still talk about a *neurodynamics* in the brain or a *mechanics* of the mind? Can we make any predictions about the trajectory our brain or mind will follow, given a set of initial conditions and inputs?

A reductionist is apt to answer "yes," and then add the qualifier "in principle." Leaving aside for the moment the question of whether a given description of neural or mental states is appropriate, can any such description be rendered, and if so, can it be predicted?

I would give a qualified "yes" to the first part of this question. If we could confine our attention to a very limited portion of the brain, we might arrive at a description that specifies what neurons are firing and in what succession. The time frame of that description would be that of an external observer, with the caveats already mentioned. But we must not underestimate the complexity of even such a limited undertaking. A single cubic millimeter of brain tissue (less than $\frac{1}{16,000}$ of a cubic inch) contains over a million neurons. To monitor the activity of each of these cells at the same time is beyond present technology. (There are methods for tracing activity over large brain areas, such as PET scans, but these give no information on the temporal details of this activity.)

How about *predicting* the dynamics of a small portion of brain tissue? Here we must admit that we are not talking only about technological difficulties, but about an impossibility *in principle*. It is important to understand this.

Physicists are much less confident today than they were in the past that the future of a complex dynamical system can be predicted, even if everything about the present state of the system can be measured with great precision. Much has been written about the uncertainties introduced into physics by quantum mechanics. But even a classical description does not always provide the ability to predict. A phenomenon called *chaos* is responsible for this lack of predictability.[4] Chaotic systems have the property that minute changes in initial conditions lead in relatively short times to very substantial differences in the trajectory of the system. There is nothing very mysterious about such systems. They may follow ordinary rules of classical mechanics and are thus said to be perfectly *deterministic*. That means that the future of such a system is predictable, providing three conditions are satisfied: The *exact* state of the system has to be known at one moment; the system has to be shielded from all disturbances from the outside; a computer of virtually infinite speed and capacity is available.

Not one of these conditions is attainable in practice. Chaotic processes typically contain instances of knife-edge decisions in which the future of the system is radically altered one way or another. The dynamics at this point are so critical, so sensitive to minute differences in conditions, that sufficiently precise measurements are totally beyond our powers.

Let the curves in the diagram below represent the trajectories of a chaotic system. Here, if the system starts out at a, it will sometime later find itself at A; if starting at b, it will go to B. In that sense the system is *deterministic*. But there is a region, C, denoted by the dotted line, where the trajectories are extremely close to each other, so close, in fact, that no practicable measurement of the state of the system in this chaotic region can distinguish them from each other. Hence we don't know which way the

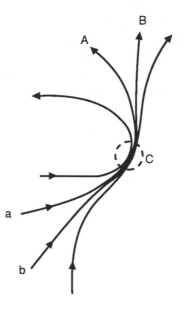

Dynamic paths in a chaotic system.

system is going. The first of the above-named three conditions therefore would require measurements of virtually infinite precision. Furthermore, the slightest disturbance of the system, when in the chaotic region *C*, may cause it to make the infinitesimal jump from one trajectory to another. Thus, even with infinite precision, no predictions can be made unless the system is isolated from all external influences. The second condition may be equally beyond reach. Every part of the universe is constantly subjected to fluctuating gravitational influences, some of which are mostly predictable, such as the forces our own sun exerts on different parts of the solar system, but the vast majority are too remote to be known to us. Unfortunately, as in the *butterfly effect* (see below), no influence, no matter how minute, can be ruled out as determining the future course of a chaotic system. As to the third condition, even if we had the ideally complete information on the present state of the system, and even if we could insulate the system against all disturbances from the outside, we would find that no present or contemplated supercomputer could use this information to compute a trajectory since, again, virtually infinite precision would be required. To say that such processes are *deterministic* is only to say, then, that they would be predictable if certain conditions were fulfilled that *can't be* fulfilled.

A simple example of a chaotic process is the game of chance pictured below. A ball dropped into the slot at *A* will soon wind up in one of the six pockets at the bottom. The outcome, which depends on the sequence of knife-edge decisions encountered on the way, is not predictable even though guided by simple Newtonian dynamics.

Another simple system showing chaos is the tumble of a pair of dice. To predict the outcome of the toss, we would have to know the velocities, spins, and initial positions of the dice as they leave our hand with a precision far beyond anything that is measurable. We would have to know the details of the surface at the points they hit, down to microscopic properties, and small disturbances of the gravitational field—and with this massive amount of data it would still take a computer of unheard-of precision to arrive at a prediction of the outcome. Any unforeseen influence, such as the feeblest air current, or perhaps the gravitational disturbance from a passing airplane miles away, could upset the whole calculation. We can say with confidence that a chaotic process such as the tumble of dice is unpredictable by any practical means.

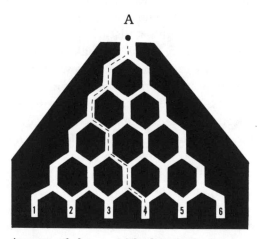

A game of chance with chaotic dynamics.

Another common example is the weather. Local conditions can actually be predicted a few days in advance with a fair degree of confidence if a large number of variables such as temperatures, barometric pressures, and cloud and wind conditions over surrounding areas are known. Predictions over longer periods of time require greater and greater precision and eventually become totally unpracticable. Meteorologists speak of the *butterfly effect*: the beat of a butterfly's wing on the other side of the globe could totally change the weather pattern in New York a few months from now. So much for the *Farmer's Almanac*.

Although it is difficult to prove that a system of many interacting neurons contains elements of chaos, it is likely that in the course of neural dynamics there occur many knife-edge decisions of the type shown in the picture of the game of chance. I have already alluded, in chapter 9, to the fact that memories must come in all grades of intensity, and that the weakest of these must constitute a noisy background to the strong associations that seem to guide the direction of our thoughts.

The presence of chaotic dynamics will make it inevitable that these faint influences, like the butterfly effect in meteorology, render long-range forecasting (anything longer than a few seconds) of our neural or thought patterns virtually impossible. It also conveys to us a picture of thought processes that is different from the conventional assumption that we simply proceed along the line of strongest stimuli and most vivid associations. I have stated previously[5] that we have a mechanism here of drawing from the inexhaustible pool of the virtually forgotten, the *minutiae* of memories and sensory input patterns.

This may be taken as an argument for *subliminal* cues. But, unlike the supposed use of such devices in advertising, subliminals, as I conceive of them, are far too numerous at every stage of the perceptual process for a single one to be useful in the control of our mental dynamics.

Physical systems, whether or not they are chaotic, obey laws that physicists have laboriously culled from nature. The laws also provide what we call *understanding* of natural phenomena. The most intuitive of these are *conservation laws*, which tell us that something remains the same throughout a physical process. Because the brain is a physical system it is subject to the same laws, but we often fail to derive a satisfactory understanding of brain function from seeing these laws operating here. Take, for example, the law of conservation of energy. It is universal, and the brain should be no exception. It tells us that in any physical system the total amount of energy must remain constant if the system is isolated from its surroundings; if not, it will increase or decrease by exactly the amount that enters or leaves from the outside.

The law is of little help in understanding brain function, even though the brain is the body's most voracious consumer of energy. But energy, in the form of glucose, is supplied liberally by the bloodstream, starving other parts of the body if necessary, so that energy is available to all parts of the brain whenever needed. Of course, the laws of electromagnetism and electrochemistry help us understand the dynamics of the action potential and its transmission across synapses; but beyond the interaction of a small number of neurons, our laws of physics give us little guidance when it comes to predicting neural dynamics.

The same is true in the world of the mind. Thoughts and memories come and go. We look in vain there for conservation laws. In Part IV we will discuss how the enormously complex and delicate network of memories and associations that we call the *self* is assembled throughout our lives. It crumbles into nothingness at the end, and sometimes long before. Freudian psychiatry was an attempt to trace through the maze of mental transactions something that remains unchanged, perhaps some childhood experiences that affect us for the rest of our lives and must be confronted because, like the incompressible fluid, they cannot be pushed out of existence. It is at best a weak conservation law. We learn and we forget, and some of the most precious of our thoughts are unexpected and untraceable.

Psychoneural Identity?

Few people would dispute the fact that a connection exists between the physical activity of neurons in the brain and the dynamics of the mind. Our capacity to think is diminished when the brain is under the influence of drugs, and no thought will cross the mind when under deep anesthesia. Most of us accept that our consciousness ceases with the death of our body. But no present theory can explain how thoughts and sensations arise from the firing of so many neurons.

ⓥⓥⓥⓥ

At one end of the spectrum of theories that attempt to connect mind and brain is the *psychoneural identity theory*, first proposed in 1967 (but later abandoned) by the American psychologist Herbert Feigl.[6]

The theory states boldly that the two realms really are one and that their nature is physical. A thought merely *is*—not *arises from*, not *accompanies*, but identically *is*—a particular spatio-temporal firing pattern of neurons in your brain. *Identity* means that the connection between the mental and the physical is rigid: same firing pattern, same thought. We should not even speak of connection, since only one thing exists, but apparently two ways of talking about it.

One difficulty arises immediately. Mental states cannot be located in time with any kind of precision, and *time* in the neural system is an ill-defined quantity. This makes it difficult even to *define* a neural state. Is a neural state the conditions of all neurons as determined by an observer if he had placed microelectrodes into all neurons? And is that state to be compared with the mental state *at that same instant*, if it could be determined?

The theory, which also goes by the names *mind-brain identity theory* and *central state materialism*, enjoyed great popularity among philosophers and neuroscientists because of its simplicity and the straightforward boldness with which it seemed to cut through the Gordian knot of the mind-brain problem. Since its first appearance it has spawned a number of modified versions that seek to overcome some of its fundamental difficulties. It is still, in one form or another, the touchstone of the orthodox materialist view.

What is being said here? When we assert the *identity* between a mental state and a neural state, we must be able to say more about the two. We know mental states, as Feigl points out, *by acquaintance*—nobody has to tell us what it is to feel sad or happy. We know *neural* states *by description*—somebody must tell us, or else we have to perform elaborate experiments to find out.

As it turns out, we are unable to quantify our mental states, or communicate them with any kind of precision, because we have no way to compare them between individuals. My *acquaintance* is limited to my own mental state. You have your headache and I have mine.

The situation with neural states is not much better. With microelectrodes we can monitor the activities of, at most, a few neurons at a time. But this is an invasive technique; to extend it to the entire nervous system is out of the question. The subject would be dead before we placed the first thousand electrodes in his brain, and we would still have many billions to go.

There are, to be sure, other techniques. Electroencephalograms are obtained by placing electrodes at many points on the scalp and recording the weak electric fields produced there by the neural activity underneath. The procedure is harmless but shows only the combined effects of the activities of many neurons. This is helpful in the diagnosis of some nervous diseases, but cannot be said to give us anything like the *state of the brain*.

Then there are the blood-flow studies in which injected radioactive materials show which regions of the brain are active under different conditions. Thus one sees a specific area in the frontal lobe (Broca's area) light up when the subject is speaking. Again, this technique shows only gross spatial distribution of neural activity, averaged over considerable intervals of time. Another technology uses a device called *SQUID* (for *S*uperconducting *Q*uantum *I*nterference *De*vice) that provides detailed maps of the magnetic fields generated by neural activity deep within the brain. With a new technique called *fast magnetic resonance imaging*, scientists are now able to obtain high-resolution pictures of the brain only seconds apart. But even this is far from seeing activities of individual neurons. The method is really a blood-flow study that shows those brain regions that consume the most oxygen. Since neural activity requires oxygen as an energy source, this is an indirect way of showing which brain areas are active.

Let us figure out just how much information we would need to obtain a complete picture of the *state of the brain*—in case you think these modern methods are bringing us close to this goal. We would want to know in every millisecond (the time it takes a neuron to fire) which of the 100 billion or so neurons are active and which are not. If we denote activity by a "1" and inactivity by "0," this would require a string of 100 billion zeros and ones every millisecond, or 100 trillion every second. To give a running account of the true neural state, I would have to produce in every second something like 110 million books, each containing a million symbols. This awesome record is to be compared with my mental states as they occur.

The enormity of the assertion contained in the psychoneural identity theory is becoming clear—but the situation is even worse than this. The individuality of each brain (see discussion in chapter 12) implies that the supposed identity is different for every person. Even if I could record both my mental and my neural states and find the correspondence between them, this could not be expected to apply to anyone else's brain. Still worse: a single brain, unlike a computer, is continuously changing its characteristics in response to its contact with the rest of the world. Unlike the computer, it can never be reset to an earlier state. It is doubtful, therefore, that the same neural state will be repeated—ever! The same thing is equally true for mental states. My frame of mind, my precise thoughts at this moment, will never return.

What, then, is the content of the identity theory? It comes down to the assertion that my mental states, which are accessible to me but impossible to communicate in any detail, and the accompanying neural states, which could be communicated (at the rate of 100 million volumes per second) but are inaccessible, are either the same thing or perhaps two aspects of the same thing, like the faces of a coin. In view of the above discussion, such a statement could never be subjected to an empirical test and has no predictive value.

Chapter 11

A Progression of Mirrors

It made the prisoner anxious, not having a pencil stub or scrap of paper. His thoughts fell out of his head and died. He had to see his thoughts to keep them coming.

Don DeLillo, *Mao II*

The Joycean Machine

What we are thinking is determined much of the time by what comes in from the outside world through our sense apparatus, and by what demands the environment makes on our attentions and actions. There are times, though, the all-too-rare quiet periods in our days, when our muscles are in repose, our senses have nothing of interest to report, and nothing needs to be done. A cat in this condition would promptly fall asleep. Humans sometimes *think*. This case of a free-running brain, as depicted in Rodin's *Thinker*, is perhaps the purest form of the thought process, the undisturbed "stream of thought" described by William James and depicted in the novels of James Joyce. Dennett calls this the *Joycean Machine*.

If you are not able to see or smell a rose right now, or feel the sting of its thorns, it is because your senses are otherwise occupied and cannot be fooled easily into reporting what isn't there. You can *think* of these things, but that is more like manipulating symbols than sensing the real thing. In your sleep, however, these images can become so palpable that they are easily confused with reality.

What is the difference between seeing a rose, thinking of a rose, and dreaming of a rose? In seeing, a true image is passed from retina to LGN and on to the cortex, where it is gradually dissembled into its various features. In *thinking*, some of the feature sensitive centers may be stimulated from above. The top-down

105

connections are there, as we have seen, at practically all levels of the sensory pathways. In *dreaming,* I believe, this top-down control reaches down farther toward peripheral sensory centers where the sensory messages are still more like pictures than codes. Thus, dreaming of a rose may cause neural activity at the LGN not unlike that caused when actually seeing one. This simulated sensory pattern is now reflected back to the cortex, where it is received *as though it had come all the way from the retina.*

Images of greater or lesser realism are formed at various levels of sensory processing by feedback from higher levels. The neural loops that generate these mental images are *creative* in the sense that they allow us to view what isn't really there and to invent what does not yet exist. But they also play a role in the perception of the world around us because they can direct our attention, enhance features deemed significant, and suppress extraneous detail. The loops are self-referent: the signaler and the perceiver are one, and we have eliminated the need for the homunculus that always bedeviled the traditional slaughterhouse paradigm of sensory processing.

The sequence of stations along the visual pathway is not unlike a progression of mirrors that receive their images both from above and from below. But the mirrors are not just passive elements. There is an interplay among reality, fancy, and chance, as on an artist's sketchpad. The outcome can never be taken for granted.

The sequence is terminated at one end by the retina, which, as long as we are awake, pours a continuous stream of images into the system. At the other end lies the bewildering neural jungle of the rest of the cerebral cortex. Dennett calls it simply the *workspace.* Here we must envision a virtually limitless variety of neural firing patterns representing a virtually limitless number of discrete ideas, concepts, memories, all in neural codes that we could not begin to decipher.

The complexity of what goes on at this level, which contains the largest number of neurons, is beyond any computational resources of present or contemplated supercomputers. The dynamics, most likely, also contain elements of *chaos,* which makes it noncomputable by any practicable means.

This hubbub of activity in the cortex cannot account by itself for a single thought. I mentioned in chapter 8 that, if the connections between brain stem and cortex were severed, we would be in a coma, insensate and unresponsive, even though sensory information could continue to flow into the cortex. We would be unconscious and unaware of this bubbly broth of cortical activities, unable to select some of them for closer scrutiny, a process that has been called *zoomability*.[1] The cortical goings-on there are *virtual* happenings, like latent images on undeveloped film, like symbols whose referents have been lost.

We spoke of the coded sensory messages at the upper levels of the sensory pathway. *Code* is really a misnomer here. The cryptogram resulting from my viewing a rose is not *decoded* by yet another brain center higher up. We can only say that there is a *correspondence* between the object and its neural expression, in that similar stimuli will elicit similar—although never identical—responses.

However, I believe that this correspondence is insufficient to account for perception. We still have to explain how replaying these central neural activity patterns will give me the sensation that a real object, a rose, is being observed.

The key to this puzzle is found in the feedback pathways that link higher to lower centers along the visual pathway. Imagine yourself an intelligent homunculus locked inside your own cranium, and watching the neural activity patterns as they devolve. If you are really observant, you may perceive certain recurrent patterns, among these one we shall call the *R pattern*. Using your wits, you may surmise that similar things are going on *out there* every time the R pattern appears.

But, what are those things? You have never seen a rose, never even seen color. "There is that R pattern again," you will say—dispassionately, because it has no beauty, no smell.

The possibility of top-down control afforded by the feedback pathways adds a new perspective to the problems of perception and of thought processes in general. The mechanisms I have proposed amount not just to an inversion of the flow of information but to an inversion of the entire sensory process: central "coded" patterns of activity are produced by sensory input, and central activity, in turn, will stimulate peripheral "sensory" patterns. This self-referent creative loop is to be accomplished by an optimization process. I describe the Alopex process, which can carry out this task, in the appendix. It has the ability to reinforce and suppress features in the incoming sensory pattern. Given bland or absent sensory input, it can start the loop from the workspace, that inexhaustible source of cognitive fragments. The feedback, driven by the optimization mechanism, will then generate progressively more pictorial representations at the various screens along the visual pathway, to be reflected back as quasi-sensory patterns to higher centers. We have seen this property in the computer simulations (illustration on page 86) in which the picture of a single face is pulled out of a workspace that contains activities corresponding to several different faces. Gerald Edelman hints at something like this when he says that the reentrant neural pathways have "a constructive function, not just a corrective one."[2]

I have pointed out before that among the numerous memories laid down in this network, there must be a background of very feeble traces that together have all the appearance of noise. We have also learned that one of the properties of chaotic processes is that they can magnify even the smallest of such fluctuations. This noise is thus potentially *semantic* because it is a rich source of unexpected and totally unpredictable turns in our thought processes.

The word *zoomability*, introduced earlier, has been used to describe this ability to focus on a germ of an idea within the teeming broth of cerebral goings-on, enlarge it, and develop it into a full-fledged thought. The English physicist Roger Penrose believes that this selection and amplification has to do with processes that in quantum mechanics are called the *collapse of the wave function.* "I am speculating," he says, "that the action of conscious thinking is very much tied up with the resolving out of alternatives that were previously in linear superposition." But quantum mechanics alone does not suffice. He further ventures that "this is all concerned with the unknown physics. . .which, I am claiming, depends upon a yet-to-be discovered theory of quantum gravity. . . ."[3]

It may well be that the *sensation* of consciousness requires some "unknown physics." However, I believe that the relatively simple self-referent mechanisms proposed here go a long way toward accounting for the selection and amplification that consciousness seems to require.

It is interesting to reflect on the question of guidance in this stream of thoughts. I think of the nascent ideas at the highest levels as *competing for expression* at the lower levels, where one idea at a time is selected and elaborated. But this selection does not make the LGN what Dennett calls "*a thalamic boss* that *understands* the current events being managed by the various parts of the brain with which it is 'in communication.' "[4] But the LGN and the other screens provide appropriate sketchpads, which enable the higher cortical levels to formulate a coherent stream of ideas and thoughts. The conscious thought is then that cooperative and unitary process that arises in the cyclic interaction between the workspace and its various reflecting screens.

Beyond the Self-Horizon

I believe that the prototype of the self-enhancing and self-referent mechanisms described above may be extended well beyond the boundaries of the individual. In chapter 8 I pointed to our predilection for creating material images in the world of objects, and I speculated that we often create these images more for our own pleasure than for that of others. In fashioning these sketches, paintings, or sculptures, we allow an often nebulous idea to initiate the creative process, which is further driven by the product that emerges under our hands.

When we show our creation to other individuals we are adding yet another layer to the progression of mirrors. The critical comments, praise, and commercial success become part of a wider loop that adds an essential ingredient to the creative act.

In my long career as university professor and researcher, I have tried on occasion to rehearse an address to be given to a special audience, or a paper to be presented at a scientific congress, sometimes to check on the timing, sometimes talking into a tape recorder to hear how it sounds. I have never really succeeded in this. Talking as though there were an audience before me not only seemed contrived, it just didn't work. Usually, after a few stilted sentences and awkward pauses, I gave up trying. It was entirely different when I confronted the real audience.

When delivering a physics lecture to a large class of students I was always aware of the attention level of the class. The fidgeting of a single student in an audience of three hundred would sometimes cause me to stop the lecture and dispatch a reprimanding look in the direction of the offender. I often wondered why I found these little distractions so annoying. But I understand now that the students were part of the loop that created the lecture, that without them I couldn't have stood there for an hour talking, gesticulating, and demonstrating, and that the *reflection* from each one of them was essential to the process.

In chapter 6 I pointed out that behaviorism could not render account of actions that are not traceable to a preceding stimulus. I mentioned creative acts in which the brain itself is the *source* of behavior. We see now that—in order to create—the brain needs as a minimum of stimulation an echo of its own nascent thought.

With language, humans have invented the most powerful means of reaching out beyond the horizon of their selves and of projecting images that may be reflected with the coloration from other individuals. But language may not have started out this way. Infants begin to talk to themselves before they talk to others, and I have ventured a guess[5] that the beginnings of language in man's history may similarly have been soliloquies rather than communication. If so, this may be compared with the apparently solipsistic expressions of paleolithic art in the caves of Spain and southern France. If I am correct, then language as we know it arose through the sharing of originally private vocabularies among larger and larger numbers of individuals.

The revolutionary effect that the beginnings of a common language must have had on the depth and range of human thought came not only from the pooling of information but from having added another layer to the progression of mirrors from which ideas are reflected. Just as the presence of attentive students shaped my lectures, so early humans must have been inspired by their listeners and become more creative in the process of presenting ideas. The transpersonal reflections eventually included such enhancing features as praise, applause, reputation, fame.

The late skating champion Sonja Henie expressed what every athlete and performing artist knows: "The give and take with the audience has a remarkable effect on one's own ability to perform." Susan Faludi, the writer on women's issues (*Backlash*, 1991), wrote of the "transformative effect" lecturing can have on the speaker. "Women need to be heard," she said, "not just to change the world, but to change themselves."[6]

Civilization has added layer upon resonating layer to the progression of mirrors that surround our individual selves. Our complex society requires us to anticipate the future and to plan, often well beyond our own life span. We write last wills and testaments, and take satisfaction in knowing that "our affairs are in order." The other morning I saw my eighty-seven-year-old neighbor, who lives alone in an old farmhouse, plant a small sapling in place of a large maple tree that was felled by an ice storm the winter before.

In his mind's eye he must have seen it as the mature tree it will eventually become, but whose real image he is not likely to see.

It is the invention of the written word that truly extended the range of our individual thoughts, and allowed us to communicate with individuals that would otherwise be beyond our reach in space and time. We do not have to hear their responses to benefit from their existence. Their presence somewhere sometime is enough to complete the loop. The writer's hope of seeing his or her thoughts in print is one of the most powerful incentives in the advancement of ideas. I would find it as difficult to write to an imaginary audience as I found it impossible to lecture to an empty auditorium. Our actions are forever embedded in the fabric of our civilization on which we try to make ripples and dream that they may spread and perhaps even propagate into the future.

Somewhat closer to home, the human search for love expresses the need for a nearby "reflector" that returns some of the warmth we are willing to give to others, and we react with a feeling of loneliness when the self is exposed to a universe that provides no echoes.

But it is not just with other humans that we communicate through the written word. What makes natural science such an absorbing activity is the hope for an occasional reflection not so much from the audience of my peers as from the subject matter of my inquiry. Science is a discourse with the universe. To observe, to experiment, is to ask questions. To put forth a theory is to challenge nature and wait for her to nod or prove you wrong. Nature is like a cloudy crystal ball in which, if we are lucky, we may detect a glint of something fitting together, a hint of order where before there was confusion. These are admittedly rare occasions, but they lead us on as we converse with a star or look, as from a distance, into our own soul.[7]

PART FOUR

THE WORLD SHE SANG

She was the single artificer of the world
In which she sang. And when she sang, the sea,
Whatever self it had, became the self
That was her song, for she was the maker. Then we,
As we beheld her striding there alone,
Knew that there never was a world for her
Except the one she sang and, singing, made.

Wallace Stevens, *The Idea of Order at Key West*

Chapter 12

The Elusive Self

*When they hear words, most
people think that there must be a message somewhere.*
Goethe, *Faust I*

We return now to take a closer
look at the *I* in light of what we covered in parts II and III. What
we find most puzzling is the feeling of selfhood, the consciousness
of being one, uniquely and nonreproducibly *one*. If this is a delusion, it is one universally shared by all humans. What, then, is the
distinction—if any—between the self-conscious *individual* and a
machine? We think in particular of that embodiment of all machines, the one that seems capable of doing anything we ask of it:
the computer. Will it, as some claim, eventually become our com-
petitor? Will we be made obsolete by the animations we created?

The word *atom* comes from the Greek *atomos*, meaning indivisible. Atoms were once believed to be particles that could not
be broken down further. They also were believed to be indestructible. But atoms have been split, quartered, smashed to smither-
eens, and even totally annihilated, by contemporary physicists.

The word *individual* comes from the Latin *individuus*, meaning indivisible. It has been widely held that an individual, a *self*,
is a unit that is an indivisible whole, although not an indestructible one. I am my *self* and *all* of my self, and nobody else can have
part of my self. But we have heard of split personalities, multiple
personalities, and—with the advent of split-brain surgery—personalities that apparently are physically as well as mentally cut in
two. Moreover, some contemporary philosophers hold that selfhood is a figment of the imagination, and that what we think is
one is really a *tribe* of little selves they call *agents*.

The feeling of selfhood of the *indivisible one* is the centerpiece of the mind-body problem. What is behind this feeling? What

115

delineates the self, and what gives it continuity throughout all the profound changes it must undergo between infancy and death? And above all, how are we to account for its consuming interest in its own perpetuation?

Let us start with the *biological self*, of which we have at least the beginnings of an understanding. Our body distinguishes readily between self and nonself. It defends itself against the invasions of harmful substances by producing appropriate antibodies. This *immune reaction* is particularly important in the defense against microbial invaders. The distinction the body makes between its own cells and foreign organisms is made on the basis of detailed molecular chemistry in the cell's makeup. The same immune reaction is at work when a body rejects foreign tissue. Blood comes in four distinct types. A transfusion of the right type may save your life. A relatively small amount of the wrong type can kill you. The body is even more selective when it comes to tissues such as skin, kidney, bone marrow, or heart. Acceptance of a skin graft can be taken for granted only among identical twins.

The biological distinction between self and nonself thus is genetically determined. We *inherit* molecular specifications that distinguish us from most other people. Fortunately for organ transplants, some duplication is allowed. There are matches. Biological selfhood is not entirely unique.

The genetically determined immunological self is modified after birth by the record of challenges to our immune system. A case of the measles will generate enough antibodies to last us a lifetime. Chances are, we will never catch the measles again. Our inherited immune personality thus is further diversified by immunological memory.

We note here that the immunological self is not simply a physical object—our body, for example—because of the body's constant exchange of material in and out of it, and the continuous renewal of virtually all of its parts. Nor is it just a process, like cell division or DNA replication. It is the *totality* of immune responses to all *potential* challenges to the individual. If I had to label the biological self with a single descriptive noun, I would call it a *potentiality*.

Choice and Selfhood

The *mental self* is unquestionably tied to the individuality of a given brain. (See discussion of identity theory in chapter 10.)

The brain, and with it the individual's mentality, evolve in parallel with the biological self. The blueprint of the brain is genetically determined like that of all other body parts. But there is one significant difference: The unspecified randomness that determines the microstructure of all tissues, and which is irrelevant in the case of liver or kidney, assumes functional significance in the brain. This means that the trillions of connections among neurons that define a brain are not specified in all detail by a person's inherited genes. Hence even identical twins have different neural nets, as they have different fingerprints. But unlike the random events that account for the irrelevant differences in fingerprints, the initially random differences in neural connectivities will in time become nontrivial features of that brain's operation, defining its own peculiar language.

Taking, then, the brain of a newborn, there are two elements that determine its precise structure: its genetic blueprint, often referred to as *nature*, and a random component. The latter may not affect such traits as intellectual and emotional predilections, but must affect the detailed neural representations of reality in the future.

From the moment of birth, and possibly before that, the native brain is subjected to a steady bombardment by sensory messages, each of which leaves behind some trace of its passage. It is believed that learning and memory consist of subtle changes in the strengths among the trillions of synapses that link neurons together. This process goes on throughout our lifetimes. Of course, it is not only the succession of messages from the outside world that changes the functioning of the brain. I have repeatedly stressed the brain's ability to elaborate new relationships between events, a process we refer to as *thinking*. Beyond that, we also recall and elaborate *thoughts*, and find new relationships between them. We are probably the only species that thinks about thinking.

It is a truism, therefore, that our brain is never the same as it was a minute earlier, hence two successive identical situations are not likely to be faced in exactly the same way. Yet, remarkably, we have the distinct impression that there remains a persistent core of selfhood that is modified, built on, but never abandoned.

The specifications our environment imposes on the brain are referred to as *nurture*, and we have all heard long and tedious arguments about the relative importance of the contributions of nurture and nature to our selfhood. The extreme positions are termed *environmental* and *biological determinism*, respectively. An advocate of environmental determinism would argue that the newborn brain is a blank sheet, a *tabula rasa*, on which the environment proceeds to write its unique story. By contrast, the biological determinist sees personality *determined*—with all the rigor this word implies—from the start by our genetic heritage. We are *born* music lovers, bums, scientists, poets, gamblers, or any combination of these and other traits.

Both viewpoints are fraught with political overtones and have been marked by some passionate controversy. The notion of the *tabula rasa* goes back to the English philosopher John Locke, became the favorite slogan in the period of the French Enlightenment, and led to the American precept that *all men are created equal*. The opposing view grew out of Darwinian evolutionary theory and ascribes all our faculties to inheritance. It had its first powerful advocate in the English writer Francis Galton and led to such undesirable outgrowths as eugenics, biological elitism, and racism.[1]

The truth almost certainly lies somewhere between the two extremes. Individual genetic determinants must have some bearing on our abilities and inclinations, and it would be very shortsighted to claim that the environment does not exert a powerful influence on the development of our minds. What neither of the above views takes into account is the transforming power of self-reference.[2] To a large extent, we are what we are, not because of genetic predilection or because of a peremptory environment, but because we have *chosen* and developed a *self-image*. Self-images, of course, may be thrust on us by the environment, but often they grow out of a multitude of factors—indigenous, mental, and environmental—that are like a noisy background in our conscious life. The environment itself, for that matter, is frequently a matter of choice.

Orthodox materialists will object that the machinery of the brain still proceeds mechanistically, and that *choice*, implying *will*, is an inappropriate term that should be expurgated. Marvin Minsky, who founded the Artificial Intelligence Laboratory at Massachusetts Institute of Technology, states categorically that "according to the modern scientific view there is simply no room at all for 'freedom of the human will.' "[3]

But what is *the* modern scientific view? Eminent theoretical physicists such as Eugene Wigner, John Wheeler, Freeman Dyson, and Roger Penrose probably would disagree with Minsky's version.

Another contemporary physicist, J. M. Jauch, remarked that causality and determinism are "in fact a gigantic prejudice which is often wrongly identified with the very essence of science."

Materialists would counter that—leaving aside the uncertainties introduced by quantum mechanics—the laws of nature are deterministic, hence what happens today is a necessary consequence of what happened before. The chain of causal necessity is solid and can be followed as far as you wish both into past and future.

Let us examine this proposition by considering a simple everyday scene. A young woman, let us call her Mary, is in a dress shop looking for something to wear on a special occasion—a party, a wedding, or a date. She picks a few dresses off the racks, tries them on, and eventually buys one of them.

Knowing Mary, we might say that over the years she has developed a certain self-image: "Low necklines don't suit me—my neck is too long." "I don't look good in green." With each dress she tries on, she checks the mirror critically. "Is this the image I am trying to project?" "How will this go over?" "Too daring? Too staid? Too expensive."

"Perfect!"

An orthodox materialist would look differently at this scene. Mary's decision to buy that dress was preordained since the time of the big bang. It could have been read in the swirling cosmic dust that was to become the planet earth five billion years ago. The neurons in Mary's brain were merely following an ancient script. All her posturing before a mirror was wholly unnecessary. Nothing could have freed her from the iron grip of determinism.

Such an opinion was expressed by the eighteenth-century French astronomer and mathematician Pierre-Simon Laplace and is known as Laplace's *world machine*. The physicist Niels Bohr described Laplace's machine as follows:

> *All interactions between the constituents of this machine were governed by the laws of mechanics, and therefore an intelligence knowing the relative positions and velocities of these parts at a given moment could predict all the subsequent events in the world, including the behavior of animals and man.*[4]

He then points out the fallacy of this picture in light of more recent developments in physics.

What the orthodox materialist thinks of as *the* scientific view is really more like the hoary *karma* of Indian mysticism or a modern version of the Greek *fates*. Recall that Oedipus was *preordained* to kill his father and marry his mother. Another young man was foolish enough to think he could avoid an appointment with death by hiding out in Samara.

But what, precisely, are we saying? Are we claiming that the future is written down somewhere, perhaps in some arcane manuscript in an ancient and forgotten language? Is fate preordained by some deity, accessible only to seers and prophets?

Here is where science and mysticism part ways, for *determinism* refers only to the nature of the process, not to its long-range outcome. True, some deterministic processes, such as the motion of the major planets in our solar system a million years hence, may readily be predicted by computing ahead. But other equally deterministic systems, such as the weather, are of a dynamic that cannot be foreseen more than a week in advance. To say that the tornado that struck here today was preordained a year ago is a meaningless statement. It was not "in the cards" or "in the stars" or in any other hidden source of knowledge. Its occurrence was not predetermined until just before it happened.

It is just as meaningless to say that Mary's choice of a dress was preordained. The precise measurements of the motion of all the particles surrounding Mary, including those making up Mary's brain, are clearly out of the question. And even if these data could be obtained, it would take a supercomputer an eternity to come up with a prediction. Why not just wait and watch Mary make up her mind? Scientific determinism becomes an argument against free will only if we confuse it with unscientific fatalism.

Physics, which should be the model of any hard-science approach, has dealt more liberally than orthodox materialists with the appearance of phenomena that are difficult to explain within existing theoretical frameworks. The concept of *randomness*, as used by the physicist, arose from the inability to assess the combined effects of large numbers of minute influences, as in the toss of dice (see discussion on page 98). It was originally thought to be just that: the result of many unknown influences that—if known—would be found to produce computable results. Newtonian mechanics buried in detail. But modern physics has taught us differently. Randomness is the very foundation of nature, and all mechanistic laws are mere superstructure.

Similarly, in neuroscience, we should be prepared to reexamine the questionable course of reductionist neurodynamics, which includes the formidable complexity of self-reference, and admit the very useful concept of individual choice, or free will. It is in the spirit of science to hope for an explanation of the phenomenon in terms of known laws and mechanisms. But it is not in the spirit of science to abjure the phenomenon. We will have more to say on this subject in the next two chapters.

Reviewing, then, what constitutes the neural basis of what we call the *self*, we can say that it contains elements of heredity, a dash of native randomness, a substantial layer of experience encoded as neural memory, and that other much overlooked ingredient, a self-image. The first two are our initial capital, like the severance pay with which a soldier is returned to civilian life; the last two accumulate gradually: experience by accretion, self-image by *deliberate* assembly. It is in connection with this deliberately assembled self-image that we make choices whose dynamics we ascribe in all practical interpersonal dealings to the individual's *free will*. No physical law is violated when we do that.

Take Me to Your Leader

I am sitting in my study thinking about this chapter. At the same time I see snow falling outside the window, and I hear my cat Catullus purring in the armchair in the corner. I may not be conscious of all these activities at the same time, but, if asked, I can report where I am sitting (and why), what I am thinking about, what I see, hear, and so forth. If you asked, what is the *thing* behind all these *I*'s, I would tend to answer that it is the same *I* in all these cases, my own *self*, but I would be hard pressed to define it for you beyond describing an intuitive feeling of oneness, autonomy, uniqueness, and a certain boundedness. The boundaries, to be sure, are not always sharp. Certainly, all parts of my body belong to me, even though many of them could be replaced by machine or transplant. But the self, as I pointed out in connection with the immunological self, is neither an object nor a process. We fail when we try to compress its attributes into a word or phrase. This does not mean that we cannot talk about it intelligently. Again, if one word is to be used, I would call it a *potentiality*. It is all the things my brain is capable of doing.

The oneness of the self is often disputed. Minsky replaces the self with countless little agents, each "mindless by itself." Together they make up what he calls the *society of mind*. He quotes a poem by the neurophysiologist Theodore Melnechuk, which ends with the lines

Still I keep a single name
labeling a twinkling sea
though it is ten billion waves
that are constituting me.

Dennett draws analogies between human selfhood, on the one hand, and ants, termites, and hermit crabs, on the other. The hermit crab adopts an abandoned snailshell to house its tender, vulnerable body. Is that shell part of its self? Ants and termites build elaborate structures. These activities appear to reflect the planning and supervision of a single mind. Ant colonies have even been said to have a *soul*.[5] Both ant and termite colonies have queens, but, as Dennett points out, these are "more like crown jewels to be protected. . .(or) much more like Queen Elizabeth II than Queen Elizabeth I. There is no Margaret Thatcher bee (ant?), no George Bush termite, no Oval Office in the anthill."

The implication seems clear. Whatever mysterious force coordinates the activities of a million ants or termites, something similar must be operating in the human brain. Dennett sees no boss inside the individual to direct the myriad agents that perform all the functions that serve that individual. The *self* is a figment of the imagination. Dennett substitutes for this nonexistent "brain-pearl" something he calls the *"center of narrative gravity"* around which we spin tales about ourselves. It is not clear, however, how this center of narrative gravity insinuates itself into my consciousness and tells me that the *I*'s that sit, think, see, and hear are all one and the same and not different agents speaking through the same mouth.

It appears that, in place of the old Cartesian dualism, we now have a radical pluralism, a million witless agents instead of one clever homunculus. It hardly seems like progress. In the process of demystifying the brain, Dennett has mystified the ant colony. But the problem of the leaderless ants is easily resolved. If it is true that the individual ants are not directed by a supervisor, then it must be true that each ant is genetically programmed to work in conjunction with its colony mates to construct that anthill according to specifications that have evolved as optimal. The startling unity of purpose and the dovetailing of efforts is achieved by the identity of the genetic programs that reside in the brain of each worker ant. This accumulated and shared evolutionary knowledge is the *Thatcher ant* that directs operations.

Let us look now at the hordes of homunculi proposed by Dennett or Minsky's mindless agents. Unlike the worker ants, they are all performing different functions. Are they programmed genetically to cooperate to work for the good of the body to which they are attached? Is there a honcho-homunculus, or do they all respond independently to the exigencies of the moment? How do they communicate? And if they are designed somehow to perform their tasks without supervision, how does all this differ from an intricate machine whose different subsystems are designed to contribute their tasks to a general complex function? The materialist has a ready answer: "There is no difference."

The idea of a multitude of agents is not so unreasonable when you consider the structure of the brain, which shows a considerable amount of compartmentalization. Different areas carry out different specific functions. There are the visual, auditory, and other sensory areas of the cortex, the association areas where channels from different senses converge and mix. There are the regions whose functions are undefined—the large areas of *uncommitted cortex* characteristic of the human brain. On the output side there are the *motor* areas that can be neatly subdivided according to the muscle groups they control. Other important brain areas are the thalamus, which channels sensory messages to the cortex; the hippocampus, which is essential in the formation of memory; the limbic system, which governs our emotions; and the cerebellum, which is responsible for coordinated muscle activity.

On a smaller scale, the cortex is built up of thousands of subunits or *modules*, columns of neurons that extend downward from the surface of the cortex to the top of the white matter.

But by far the most prominent feature of the brain is its dual nature. If we look under the skull we find two identical-looking brain halves, the left and right *hemispheres*. They are connected by a massive cable of some 200 million axons, called the *corpus callosum*, that makes sure that the left brain "knows" what the right brain is doing, and vice versa. The two brain halves and the underlying corpus callosum are depicted in Vesalius's famous drawing on page 40.

Sensory messages generally go to the brain half opposite to the side from which they are received. In vision, for example, the left half of the visual field (as seen by both eyes) is sent exclusively to the right brain half. Similarly, each brain half controls the muscles on the opposite side of the body. The two brain halves thus seem to have identical functions, differentiated only with regard to the side they are serving. This symmetry is not perfect, however. Most of us are more adept at developing manual skills with the right hand, and some muscles, such as the ones controlling head and eye movements, are operated by the left hemisphere only.

The apparent symmetry was further disrupted by the French neurologist Paul Broca's discovery in 1861 that the ability to produce speech is located in the left hemisphere in a small cortical area of the frontal lobe, now called *Broca's area*. A few years later the German neurologist Karl Wernicke discovered that speech comprehension similarly depended on an area in the temporal lobe also located in the left hemisphere. These findings, together with the usual right-handedness, led to the concept of a *leading*, or *dominant*, left hemisphere. Many brain scientists assigned all the higher functions, especially consciousness, to the left brain half, but others pointed out that the right half also had its own special talents. At any rate, the corpus callosum makes sure that in the normal intact brain the two halves operate in close cooperation and with some unity of purpose and function.

Still, some prominent psychologists believe this unification is largely illusory. Michael Gazzaniga, who is best known for his extensive work with split-brain patients (see below), expresses a view not unlike Dennett's or Minsky's, saying that "the mind is not a psychological entity but a sociological entity, being composed of many submental systems. It is the uniqueness of man. . .to verbalize and, in doing so, create a personal sense of conscious reality out of the multiple systems present."[6]

Dividing the Indivisible One

The first transection of the corpus callosum in a live human was carried out in the early 1940s in an attempt to relieve the symptoms of severe epilepsy. The operation at first was only moderately successful, but when perfected a few years later turned out to be of great benefit in cases that could not be controlled by other means. A remarkable result of these procedures—considering the magnitude of the surgical invasion—was the absence of obvious behavioral symptoms following the operation. Two hundred million neural fibers connecting the two brain halves were severed and the patients appeared to be normal.

It took careful studies by psychologists Roger Sperry and Michael Gazzaniga at California Institute of Technology to bring out the subtle but profound changes caused by the operation. Without the connecting bridge, the two hemispheres acted independently in most respects, each side unaware of the sensory information received by the other. What made the startling difference, once it was noticed, was that the right brain half, the mute one, could not inform the experimenter what information it had received, and the left, the talking hemisphere, was ignorant of information going to its twin. If the patient was shown a picture of a spoon in the left half of the visual field, only the right brain half would *know*. The left, talking hemisphere would report seeing nothing. But the patient would be able to select with his left hand, from a collection of objects, the object shown. The picture of the spoon had gone to the right cerebral hemisphere, which could direct the left hand to find the match. In that sense, the right hemisphere *knew* and understood what was shown. It just lacked the ability to talk. If you are talking with a split-brain person, you are conversing with his or her left hemisphere.

Not only did the two brain halves display different knowledge of the world, they were also shown to be capable of different wants, and occasionally displayed evidence of conflict between them. Are there, then, two personalities, two free wills, two *selves* where there used to be only one?

The most radical answer was given some time ago by the philosopher Roland Puccetti, of Dalhousie University in Halifax, Nova Scotia. Puccetti not only believed that the body of the split-brain patient harbors two selves complete with separate consciousnesses, memories, associations, and wills, but that even in the normal human being the two are not integrated. Instead there lives in each of us a silent partner who constantly sees his or her desires thwarted by a more powerful companion.

The thought of a silent population of frustrated doppelgängers living alongside us is disquieting. Puccetti[7] says that it is in the nature of the cortex "to deny at all cost the presence in the same cranium of that congenital aphasic who sometimes survives us after massive left-sided lesions." The belief in this kind of duality of mind in the normal brain is generally discounted by most neuroscientists. Still, it is hard to dismiss it completely. I remarked previously on this point:

> *Perhaps I could ask my silent partner to confirm his presence by some simple gesture. "If you are there, raise our left arm!" Nothing happens. If the arm goes up, it is because I (left brain-half I) will it to do so. It is no use. My doppelgänger, if he exists, is used to letting me handle all decisions.*[8]

The late English neuroscientist Donald MacKay doubted that anything like a radical bisection of mind and consciousness resulted from split-brain surgery. He views the brain as representable by the letter *Y.* The upper two branches are the two cortical hemispheres, which are, in the normal brain, connected by the corpus callosum (the broken horizontal bar in the diagram). The lower branch of the Y stands for such deeper brain structures as the limbic system, which are not affected by the operation. It is there, he believes, that a single *"self-supervisory system"* is located, which confers unity on the individual even with the corpus callosum severed.[9]

Beam Me Up, Scottie!

The split-brain operations and subsequent psychological studies of the patients have brought out a wealth of information about the human mind. They also, we are told, have been of great therapeutic value. They have *not* told us where in the brain to look for the seat of selfhood, and whether we are dealing with one or a horde of agents.

Let us remember that we are not discussing something that is already defined. We are not describing the faults and virtues of a certain model of automobile or the properties of an atom of zirconium. In both these cases there is no question of what is meant by the object under discussion. Here, instead, we are defining the object only by discussing it. In doing so we must be careful to avoid inconsistencies, and not let the object stray too much from what is commonly *felt* to be its nature.

MacKay's picture of the brain of split-brain patients. The upper two branches of the Y represent the two cerebral hemispheres; the horizontal bar, the corpus callosum, *here shown severed. The lower branch of the Y represents lower brain centers.*

We cannot talk about mind without talking about *feelings*, a term that is frequently shunned by scientists. I see feelings as thought patterns that—unlike sensations or perceptions—do not arise from specific and present sense data. Instead, they are brewed from stored and perhaps innate knowledge, often with a dash of hormonal seasonings. Thus I would say that I may have a *sensation* of being cold, a *perception* of an approaching thunderstorm, but *feelings* of joy, apprehension, or love. This terminology is perhaps arbitrary, but it will be helpful. I can be aware or unaware of sensations and perhaps also of pereceptions, but *feelings* seem to imply awareness. We will talk more about this in the next chapter. We know next to nothing about the neural mechanisms involved in feelings, but that does not make them less real.

There is one aspect of selfhood that we have not yet considered. It has to do with a *feeling* of concern for the existence and well-being of a particular human being. Of course, we may have such a concern about many people around us. But there is *one* who is both object and agent of this concern. This relationship defines for every human a unique person who to him or her is *felt* to be the self.

Suppose we try, then, to identify the preservation of the self with the continuation of this *feeling* of selfhood, or at least the potential for such a feeling, since we don't always contemplate our selves. We may ask, "What is the prerequisite for such continuation?"

If your mental self, like your biological self, is to be associated with your unique potentialities that are in turn based on your unique brain, then the preservation of that brain in a functioning state appears to be one such prerequisite. Granted, there are degrees of preservation. Age or disease may erase part of the past and dim our perception of the present. To that extent our selfhood is also diminished.

The idea of cloning suggests itself. Biological cloning duplicates only genetic heritage. What we would need to duplicate a selfhood is a duplication of all physical details of a functioning brain that would encompass not only all genetic and random features present at birth, but also the modifications made by all subsequent experiences. The question is often raised, "*What if* we succeeded in accomplishing such duplication?" We would have to assemble another brain, molecule by molecule, using your brain as template, but without disturbing your brain. Would there now be two *yous*? It is always tricky to discuss a situation that is far removed from present possibilities. *What if* what I proposed is physically impossible? Would the question still be legitimate? This is again the contrafactual dilemma.

But suppose it could be done. Would you then have any objection to reversing the action and having your alter ego rubbed out again? Would you care if the rubbing out were done on the original you instead of on your clone? If you do, why should you?

The Oxford philosopher Derek Parfit discusses *teleportation*, a common device in science fiction, in which an astronaut is rubbed out in one place and reassembled from new material at a distant location.[10] The reassembly is controlled by a sophisticated machine that made a record of the location of every molecule in the astronaut's body before he or she was dematerialized. The persons *beamed up* always appear to be the same before and after, and none the worse for the experience. Also, they enter the teleportation chamber without hesitation, knowing that the machine will safely transport them through space and time.

But I wonder what would happen in the following scenario. Suppose Mr. Spock stepped into the chamber, and the machine succeeded in making his copy on some other planet but failed to eliminate the original. The mistake is soon discovered and the original Mr. Spock is asked to report to the captain so he can be properly dematerialized. As the captain raises his disintegrator, the astronaut pleads:

SPOCK: Hold it, captain. I'm your trusted crew member and friend. You can't kill me now. This is murder.

CAPTAIN: Be reasonable, Spock. You are not here. You are *there*. Besides, this won't hurt a bit.

Following our earlier discussion, we would have to say that—if our procedure were possible as described—we indeed would have preserved all of the person's potentialities. We must presume that the new person now has a feeling of selfhood very similar to that of the former self who disintegrated a moment earlier on another planet. But is it the same self? Or was one person killed in the process and a *different self* created?

The situation is farfetched, but it has interesting parallels in the real world. What happens when we undergo deep anesthesia? The conscious functioning of our brain is temporarily suspended. We have no sensations, no thoughts. But the potentialities are preserved in a *virtual* self that is reactivated when we emerge from unconsciousness. Our feeling of selfhood returns. Having questioned the true selfhood of a clone or teleported astronaut, we also may question whether the reawakened self is the same as the one before surgery. And, going a step further, can we be sure that *I* am the same *I* this morning as the one who went to bed last night? Or is it just that we think the same and feel the same because we are based in the same brain? We can carry this argument even further and ask whether, as we take a simple walk, our body isn't just disappearing from one place only to reappear in another, a continuous kind of teleportation. Is every step we take a near-death experience? Perhaps, as Parfit puts it, "ordinary survival is about as bad as being destroyed and having a Replica."[11]

Parfit describes the controversy between the *ego theory* and the *bundle theory* of selfhood. According to the ego theory, what makes an experience *my* experience is the existence of an *ego* apart from my physical brain and all of its recorded experiences. The ego comes first. In the course of time, a life and experiences become attached to it.

If we believe in such an ego, then our clones would have to be soulless automata, because the machine that duplicates the body, atom by atom, is not designed to duplicate egos. For the same reason, teleportation of the physical body could not guarantee continuation of selfhood. By now the starship *Enterprise* is run by zombies.

Parfit does not subscribe to this dualist view, but suggests that the essence of the self is a *bundle* of experiences running through

an individual's life. The brain, by mechanisms not further specified, attaches a *unity* to the bundle. On the bundle theory, dupli-
cating the brain would duplicate the bundle, hence create two
selves, both justly claiming to be the original person. Each would
be equally concerned about his or her continued well-being but
would consider the other as *another* person, a doppelgänger, an
impostor. To keep things simple, the teleporter should always de-
materialize one body while creating the other, and Mr. Spock will
always remain the same lovable Mr. Spock.

Selfhood, according to the bundle theory, thus is grounded in
an enormous store of organized information that in principle could
be preserved in different ways. This brings up another question.
If we could collect all of a person's past experiences and thoughts
and store them in a computer memory, we should then have a *virtual self* that, like the sleeping or drugged brain, contains all the
potentialities of that person. We do not yet have a person. A record
by itself does not play music. It only stores it.

But why couldn't we then transfer all this information to a
brain or brainlike structure and produce a feeling, self-conscious
human being? And wouldn't that be a way of extending our own
mortal selfhood? Perhaps even a cleverly constructed machine
made of many silicon chips could receive this store of personal
experience, and through built-in creative loops translate sensations
into perceptions, generate thoughts and feelings, among them the
feeling of being a single, continuous, unique, and indivisible self.
What I have described here is similar to a fantasy by O. B. Hardison
who envisions a human mind embodied in virtually immortal silicon creatures.[12]

❂❂❂❂

I have an uneasy feeling, however, that something is wrong
with this picture. The idea of storing, or *downloading*, all of the
specifications of a mature brain in some inert form—the *virtual
self*, as I called it—is an image taken from computer science where
a program can be stored in many different ways, including being
written on a piece of paper. Only when this program is loaded on
a computer will it be able to run. Similarly, I implied that when
information specifying the virtual self is run on a brain (or equivalent device), a real dynamic self will emerge. The tacit assumption here is that, as on a computer, we can neatly separate storage

from execution—in other words, the *software* of experience from the *hardware* that runs it. In the spirit of that metaphor, the brain is called *wetware* in computerese.

I believe the metaphor is flawed. A naive, untutored brain is not just like a computer that is ready to run any program we may wish to load into it. Even if we subscribe to the theory of the *tabula rasa*, we must keep in mind that every individual's brain is a different system because of the random elements it contains. The information we try to transfer is specific to the brain on which it grew in the first place. It cannot just be lifted from one brain like a computer file and downloaded on another. To run the stored software of a lifetime of experiences and thoughts, we would need a system that—unlike the general purpose computer—is matched to the stored information, a brain equivalent that not only is genetically identical to the original brain, but contains all the myriad random modifications of its circuitry that occur between conception and maturity. The amount of information necessary to specify this system is astronomical. That even a small portion of it could be extracted from a living brain without destroying it is doubtful.

Chapter 13

The Wedge of Consciousness

*In dealing with the problem
of consciousness, physicists have had courage but no competence, biologists have had competence but no courage.*

F. J. Dyson

Do we still have a mind-body
problem, or is it solved by the software/hardware analogy of the
computer? Or perhaps it was never more than Gilbert Ryle's per-
snickety "ghost in the machine."[1] It may simply be that, as Bertrand Russell assured us long ago, "by analyzing physics and
perception the problem of the relation of mind and matter can
be completely solved."[2]

Still, the chasm that separated brain science from mind science
continued to be an embarrassment to both. For many years serious
neuroscientists avoided the most challenging phenomenon exhibited by the brain: consciousness. Only very recently has there been
an upsurge of attempts to connect the mental with the physical.
Philosophers, too, have made important contributions. Prominent
among these is the thought-provoking *Consciousness Explained*,
by Daniel Dennett of Tufts University.[3]

The key to the mystery, according to Dennett, is that the individual *I*, the supposedly *indivisible* seat of my consciousness, was
never a *unit* to begin with but is made up of many busy demons
occupied with diverse tasks, similar to the *society of mind* described earlier by Marvin Minsky.[4]

The apparent unitarity of the *I* and its consciousness is largely
a delusion, according to Dennett. There is in the brain no single
stage on which the multiple events picked up by our senses are
displayed together, no *Cartesian Theater*. A multiplicity of analyzers examine what is reported by the senses, and come up with

133

multiple drafts. Dennett's model is elaborate, persuasive, and solidly grounded in an up-to-date knowledge of neuroscience.

The brain, according to Dennett, is a *virtual machine*—that is, a computerlike device made smart by appropriate software. It is the software, which is the result of our life's experiences, that enables the brain to perform all its remarkable, but still machine-like, functions.

What Is Consciousness?

If all this still leaves us less than completely satisfied, we should ask ourselves whether we perhaps are caught in a linguistic trap, trying to find the true meaning of words like *mind* and *consciousness*.

But meanings are conventions. By convention we understand words like chair, or flowerpot, or grandfather clock. But some conventions have never been clearly established. It seems there should be an easy way out of this dilemma. We must *define* our terms before we can argue about them.

This turns out to be a snare and a delusion. Some things should not be defined. Our compulsion to define things often stems from the fact that a concept, although well known, is poorly understood. It has been almost an article of faith that in such cases a definition will clear the air. In fact it will only add to the muddle. We all know, for example, what it means to be alive, but we do not understand *life*. It is absurd to expect the verbal exercise of definition to add anything we didn't know before.

Then there is the matter of precision. Life has fuzzy boundaries both at its beginning and at its end; witness the passionate controversies surrounding abortion and euthanasia. Also, when we contemplate the most primitive life forms we find again that we are unable to draw a sharp line between animate and inanimate matter. We try to remedy this situation by carefully worded definitions, only to be trapped in *if. . .then* dilemmas: *if* we call this thing live, *then* such-and-such is live whether we like it or not. We may be forced to call crystals live because they grow and multiply, and worker ants dead because they don't; or computers live because they answer our questions, and autistic children dead because they don't.

Consciousness, too, has fuzzy boundaries, and trying to impose sharpness cannot add insight. There are two broad meanings of the word I would like to distinguish, however. One has to do with the *responsiveness* of a person. Following a severe trauma, the question is often raised whether the patient is *conscious*. The answer is affirmative if he or she responds intelligently to questions. But there are degrees. There may be confusion or even the inability to answer verbally, in which case a mere nod may be taken as indication of *some* consciousness.

The second meaning is more introspective and *relational*. The statement "I am conscious of something" posits a relationship between the self and events that may be external or internal. Thus I may be conscious of your presence or of my *thinking* of you. This relational consciousness, sometimes called *subjective awareness*,[5] is the subject of this chapter.

Even with this restriction it is impossible to grasp consciousness in its entirety, and—rather than introducing questionable definitions—I will rely on the reader's own introspective familiarity with the subject. In the following pages I will discuss some attributes of consciousness. I will be successful in this approach if you recognize these as part of your own conscious experience.

This brings up another point: we ascribe conscious experience to another person in what Bisiach[6] called "introspection by proxy." We do this not to explain the other's behavior, but as an axiomatic statement relating to the very nature of consciousness.

In the end I will offer my own attempt to account—if not for consciousness itself—at least for some of its attributes. I do this in the spirit of Gerald Edelman's suggestion[7] that one must continue to try constructing a "biologically based" theory that links consciousness with neural processes, and that, even if such a theory was proved wrong, it would be of value in demonstrating the feasibility of such an effort. I also admit being motivated by what he called—and by what I think he meant by—*Cartesian shame*.

Is Consciousness Real?

With greater or lesser adroitness we are able to put the contents of our consciousness into words. I can describe what I see or hear. To each such sensation belongs a physical object or property: light or sound waves picked up, respectively, by the rods and cones of the retina and hair cells in the organ of Corti of the inner ear. Similarly, heat and cold receptors in the skin respond to temperature. But what about the sensation of pain? It is not *more heat* or *more pressure* that is felt by a person conscious of pain. The thing sensed when in pain is *pain itself*. Since pain is not a physical object or property, I will call it a *feeling* rather than a sensation. In a similar way, I am made aware of my emotional states. They can be conveyed but not defined. They need not be defined. To be angry is to *feel* anger. Anger, like pain, is not a physical object. It is—in my nomenclature—*felt*, not sensed.

In chapter 8, I described *perception* as the elaboration of sensory messages, using stored information and reasoning as a basis. Perception is thus something beyond sensation. The sensation of a loud popping noise may be perceived—depending on the circumstances—as either the backfiring of a truck engine or a gunshot.

What is the meaning, then, of being *conscious* of a sensation? Perhaps consciousness is nothing other than the arrival of sensory information at certain (higher) brain centers. Is to be conscious of a chill in the air merely having your cortex informed of that fact so as to react appropriately to the information? It turns out that we are able to answer that question, and that the answer is *no*. Subjective awareness is something beyond being informed, and the distinction is brought home by a phenomenon called *blindsight*.

The paradoxical name was coined by the Oxford physiologist L. Weiskrantz, who studied the visual capabilities of patients with damage to parts of the visual area V1 in the cortex. We recall that the chief visual pathway in humans goes from retina via LGN to V1, and from there to other cortical areas (see diagrams on pages 58, 64, and 65). Destruction of part of V1 causes blindness over corresponding areas of the visual field. Thus, if an area in V1 of the right hemisphere is missing because of surgery or disease, the patient will not be able to see objects placed within a certain region of the left half of the visual field.

Most of Weiskrantz's observations were carried out on a patient, D.B., whose surgery on V1 of the right hemisphere made him blind over virtually the entire left half of the visual field. Nevertheless, Weiskrantz found that D.B. was able to point in the direction of a flashing light within the blind area, even though he maintained that he didn't see it. Even more impressive was a series of tests in which different light patterns were flashed on a screen well within D.B.'s blind region. When *X*s and *O*s were presented in random order and D.B. was urged to guess the pattern, he achieved an almost perfect score, while still maintaining that he saw nothing.[8]

The experiments with D.B. were continued over a number of years and always yielded the same results: The light pattern projected into the patient's blind field caused no awareness on his part, and yet information was clearly received by his brain.

D.B.'s case is not unique. Similar results have been published by other research groups, and the results are reinforced by earlier observations that monkeys whose cortical areas V1 were removed entirely were nevertheless capable of acting on visual cues and successfully avoided obstacles placed in their path. Of course, we do not know anything about consciousness or its absence in other than human subjects, but it is clear that here, too, the interruption of the main visual pathway *"retina-LGN-V1-. . ."* did not block visual information from reaching the monkey's brain.

The Mysterious Monitor

The phenomenon of blindsight would be mysterious were it not for the fact that the *retina-LGN-V1* chain is not the only visual pathway. If you go back now to the diagram on page 65, you will notice a path indicated by $+ - + -$, which branches off the optic nerve between retina and LGN. This path continues to neural structures in the midbrain and is part of the remnant of an older visual system that predates the evolution of the pathway that goes through the LGN. Recently it was found also that there are neural connections from the LGN to higher cortical areas bypassing V1.

There is thus no mystery about how visual information can reach the brain, even without V1. But the remarkable fact is that this information, although usable, is not accompanied by any feeling of awareness. There evidently is, as Weiskrantz puts it, a "straightforward and unambiguous route from stimulus to response, in the absence of 'thought.' "

What is missing in blindsight, according to Weiskrantz, is a *monitoring system* that has become *disconnected*. The human subjects, while making the correct choices, maintain that they see nothing and are guessing only because they are urged to do so. Subjective awareness thus is not a necessary by-product of sensory information reaching the brain. This makes consciousness a real phenomenon, and the question, how it comes about, a legitimate scientific question.

Weiskrantz believes that there is a monitoring system that observes the rest of the brain. This popular idea goes back over

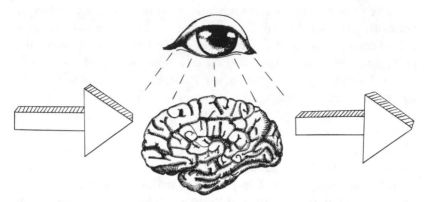

A monitoring system observing the sensorimotor brain.

a hundred years to the English biologist C. Lloyd Morgan. It is again expressed by N. Humphrey, who said: "Imagine that a new form of sense organ evolves, an 'inner eye,' whose field of view is not the outside world *but the brain itself*."[9] It is thought also that the same monitoring system carries within itself a *model of the world* and a *model of itself*, both being constantly revised, while being used to judge events observed in the lower, working parts of the brain.

The main trouble with this picture is that we know of no part of the brain that can be identified as the monitoring system or seat of consciousness, which leaves us again with the uncomfortable specter of the Cartesian homunculus.

Four Attributes

Before presenting an alternative model, I want to discuss some of the attributes of consciousness that can be readily identified. Perhaps the most striking of these are its *selectivity, exclusivity, chaining*, and—I believe—*unitarity*. The four are certainly connected, but let me explain them one by one.

1. *Selectivity.* Not all neural activities enter consciousness. Indeed, only very few do. Some of these are sensations, conveyed, for example, by the receptors in the eyes, but also by sensors located deep within our bodies. We also select into consciousness perceptions, the identified or otherwise analyzed sensory events; and feelings, the less sensory and more cerebral transactions I spoke of on page 127. In this spirit, I would call consciousness itself a feeling. Finally, we may be conscious of our own consciousness

in what has been termed a potentially infinite regress. Some hierarchy of conscious events seems to suggest itself here.

2. *Exclusivity.* Events are selected singly into consciousness. Being conscious of one thing prevents us from thinking of another at the same time. This is what I mean by *exclusivity.* The brain can simultaneously carry out hundreds of tasks—it controls your heart rate, your respiration, the widening and contracting of the pupils of your eyes, and a host of other autonomic muscular and glandular functions, while directing your arm and leg muscles to maneuver an automobile through heavy traffic. But your consciousness can accommodate only one sensation or perception or thought at a time.

A simple but striking example of this is the Necker cube below, which is perceived in one of two geometrical configurations, but never both at the same time. A similar exclusivity appeared in the perception of the face-vase pattern shown on page 63.

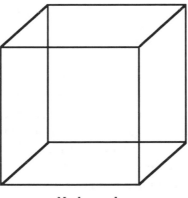

Necker cube.

3. *Chaining.* Items in consciousness are chained together, sometimes haphazardly, sometimes following a plot, linked together by association and reasoning. There may be gaps in this *stream of consciousness*, but one of the outstanding features is the serial character of consciousness.

4. *Unitarity.* The last of my four attributes is probably the most difficult to explain and the one that is most controversial. It has, I believe, a dual aspect. Consciousness unifies both the subject and the object, both the person who possesses it and the contents of his or her conscious mind. We already discussed the unity

of the self in the last chapter. Consciousness makes it appear that a single individual, not a horde of half-witted homunculi, is the recipient of all sensations, perceptions, and feelings, and the originator of all thoughts. It provides the continuity of our selfhood throughout our life span and across the gaps of dreamless sleep and other forms of unconsciousness. At the same time, it weaves the contents of the mind into a whole, making a waterfall out of a million gravity-driven droplets and a year out of billions of solitary moments. Consciousness is the *joiner* of the countless bits and pieces in the world around us. We take ten billion galaxies, each containing ten billion suns, and call it *one*. One *universe*. We then seek laws that are both *universal*, like the law of gravitation, and *unified*, like the yet to be discovered law that governs gravitation and all other forces of nature.

۞۞۞۞

There has been much speculation about the function of consciousness and its survival value. When and how has it evolved, and in response to what adaptive advantages?

The fact that single events are selected from among many, and selected to the exclusion of others, suggests that these privileged activities receive a treatment and attention not accorded the myriad other transactions the brain is engaged in.

The chaining of items selected for conscious treatment allows us to establish and consider connections between past and present events, to extrapolate into the future, and to develop flexible strategies. It gives us our capacity to reason, to present arguments, and to consider those presented to us.

Unitarity establishes the organism as a unit, an individual, navigating in a comprehensible world.

Meanwhile, the many unconscious neural activities are carried out according to genetically determined instructions, or as learned reactions to sensory inputs. They proceed virtually automatically, as in a reflex; in fact, they are sometimes called *cortical reflexes*. The difference between a simple knee jerk and bringing your car to a halt at a red light is that the latter requires learning and involves much larger neural masses. The unconscious brain is like a *logical engine* whose orderly and predictable progress is diverted only by noise and malfunction. It comes closest to the orthodox materialist's picture of a very intricate but thoroughly deterministic machine. The *conscious* brain is very different.

The Model

The idea of a cerebral monitoring system has a great deal of intuitive attractiveness. It can be made to account for the attributes listed above. But it is, as we have seen, a logical dead end. We would need a structure, an intelligent observer, the *inner eye*, which does not seem to exist in the brain. Then there is the phenomenon of *regress* already mentioned: I can be conscious of my own feeling of being conscious of something. This cycle may go on and even involve another person's consciousness. I may, for example, be aware of my belief that he thinks that I think that he is guilty of something. Here we need a whole hierarchy of inner eyes, some trained on someone else's brain. (It takes a human brain to be paranoid.)

The alternative model that is being developed throughout this book is the result of work that I carried out over the past two decades in collaboration with some of my doctoral students. It is based on the principle of pattern generation by cortical feedback as described in chapter 9. We began with the development of a particularly effective optimization procedure (see the appendix) that we used in experiments on vision and that led to the hypothesis that similar mechanisms may be operating in the brain. A number of studies followed in which computers were used to simulate the proposed neural mechanisms in a variety of situations that mimicked perceptual and cognitive tasks.

I want to account here for some of the attributes of consciousness, but I do not have a physicalist model for the feeling of being conscious and therefore cannot claim to have an *explanation* of consciousness. The attributes I have in mind are less mysterious than they seem. My model requires no separate monitoring system or "new form of sense organ," but it accomplishes the same tasks through simple and plausible neural mechanisms that are integral parts of the brain's main sensory pathways.

Much of the model has to do with the dynamics of thought processes discussed in chapter 11. I briefly recall the main features here. Central to the model is the assertion that the sensory processes that translate an incoming picture into some central, symbolic, neural activity can be *inverted*. The thought of a sensory event, originating fortuitously or through associations somewhere in the cortex, can bring about its representation in a form that is closer to the senses. This can be accomplished through an optimization process, leading to what has been called *zoomability*. The resulting *picture-in-the-head* then functions like a sensory input. What we have is a self-referent loop. The infinite regress of consciousness arises then in the most natural way as echoes between pairs of reflecting planes. Similarly, any sensory input is not just *processed* in sequential fashion like a slaughtered pig, but *iterated*, tossed back and forth, multiply reflected.

Unlike reflections by passive mirrors, the optimization process enhances the picture on every reflection and adds to its significance. The mirrors are *active*.

In this picture, consciousness involves the cyclic reactivation of images or other cognitive states through active reflection from higher order cerebral centers. The chaining of images is achieved by associative connections in the cortex, which trigger new concepts or ideas to be fed into the self-referent loops. Edelman invokes a similar picture when he says that "the possibility of re-entering signals in a recursive fashion to a lower order mapped input after they have been processed in several higher order maps is an enormously powerful way of creating new function."[10]

My model further assumes that the central, *symbolic* neural activities by themselves are not accompanied by feelings of consciousness. Many such activities must be going on simultaneously in all parts of the cortex. But subjective awareness results only when specific activities are selected for elaboration and reinforcement by self-referent channels. The visual messages coming through the old midbrain pathway, or otherwise bypassing V1, apparently have no access to these channels, hence patients with lesions in V1 exhibit the symptoms of blindsight. The individual conscious self is unaware of what is known in its cortex.

The normal visual pathway in humans consists, as we have seen, of a series of feedback loops, the most peripheral being between LGN and V1 (see diagram on page 65). Here the exclusive selection of specific sensory features is accomplished by optimization processes of the type shown in the appendix. I have demonstrated that the necessary neural mechanisms exist in the case of vision.[11] Analogous neural circuitry exists in other sensory pathways.

Let us see how this mechanism might carry out what is perhaps the most common task faced by the nervous system, and one that is particularly difficult for machines to imitate: *pattern recognition*. Suppose you are trying to spot the presence of a tank in

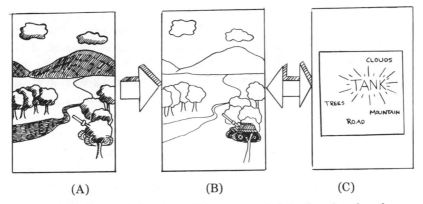

(A) (B) (C)

A scenery (A) containing a tank is represented in the visual pathway (B) with the tank reinforced through the self-referent loop involving "tank detectors" at higher levels in the cortex by top-down *control (C).*

a complex landscape. (I have chosen the example of a tank for reasons that will become obvious in the next chapter.)

If you were not specifically looking for it, you might easily be unaware of it, because it is some distance away and partially hidden by foliage. But if you are *looking for* a tank, the neural circuits in your cortex that normally become active when you see a tank—let us call them *tank detectors* for want of a better name—become *primed*. This may mean increased sensitivity or some faint activity, or both. This response is picked up and enhanced by the self-referent loop, as we saw in the computer simulation on page 86 or in the search for Napoleon on page 69. This process will boost both the strength and your awareness of the presence of the tank in the landscape before you.

We come back once again to the question of unitarity of the *I* and the uniqueness of its consciousness. If the LGN is a kind of sketchpad, as I suggested in chapter 9, the cortex exerts its top-down control by an optimization process. In this inversion of sensory processing, a pattern is selected from among many competing possibilities and drawn on the sketchpad. This selection excludes other alternatives by virtue of its bootstrap character. Many factors contribute to this selection. Among these are the raw sense data that are received, expectations based on preceding events, stored knowledge, and random fluctuations.

The process of exclusive selection that we have seen in the computer simulation experiments (page 86) is able to provide the unitarity of cognition that has been sought vainly by placing an intelligent monitor at the top of the sensory pyramid. But there is neither a theater there, as Dennett correctly points out, nor a homunculus observer to watch the plot. Dennett and others conclude from this that no unification takes place. Cognition is the production of multiple drafts; consciousness, a shared property of a horde of homunculi.

These conclusions appear to be inevitable but challenge our intuition, which favors a unitary *I*. In the present, self-referent model that I have proposed, there *is* a theater, and the action on its stage is being scrutinized by an observer. Unlike previous attempts that have placed the theater at the highest level of cerebral activity, I believe that the unification is located at the only place where sensory patterns are still whole and preserve the spatial relations of the original scene—at the bottom of the sensory pyramid, not at the top. It is there that all the sensory cues and the cerebral fancies conspire to paint a scene. There is also an observer: it is the rest of the brain looking down, as it were, at what it has wrought. Consciousness, which arises in this self-referent process, not only unifies the immediate sensory messages but also becomes the joiner of everything around us, past, present, and future.

Chance with a Purpose

I described the unconscious brain as being a kind of *logical engine*, or deterministic machine. Consciousness has the capacity to break the causal chains. The infinitesimal moment that is the present, the sliding point in time that separates past from future—but also forms the bridge from cause to effect—is replaced by a universe of self-referent activity. We can locate physical events in time. It makes sense to ask where a fast-moving bullet is at a given moment. But it makes no sense to speak of the state of my consciousness *at this instant*. This may be related to our inability to define a rigorous time scale for neural events (see discussion on pages 90–95). Caught on film by a brief flash, a speeding bullet is still a bullet, but an instant of consciousness is an empty canvas. This is just another way of expressing what Francis Bacon meant some four centuries ago when he said that "human understanding is unquiet; it cannot stop or rest."[12] Consciousness is not a point in time. It straddles broad sections of the past and reaches out into the future. Edelman speaks of consciousness as a *"remembered present"* in which "previous memories and current activities of the brain interact."

Consciousness is like a wedge driven between the *whence* and the *hence*, a timeless region where intentionality, volition, and creativity are spawned. The sources that feed into these loops may be sensory inputs that then are modified by the system. We saw examples of that in the illustrations on pages 69 and 70. Other sources are concepts, nascent ideas, originating at higher cognitive levels, for example, through associations, that then generate images.

Finally, in the truly quiescent environment, or in one we are able to ignore, the cerebral dynamics may be affected by fluctuations of neural activity that may be compared to turbulence in a fluid. I pointed out before that these fluctuations contain bits of old memories and associations of different strengths, the faintest ones blending into and becoming part of the neural background noise. Any one of these may be admitted into the self-referent loops and, once selected, will be amplified and lead to further elaboration and imagery.

The French postmodernist philosopher Jean-François Lyotard describes the process:

> *In what we call thinking the mind isn't "directed" but suspended. You don't give it rules. You teach it to receive. You don't clear the ground to build unobstructed: you make a little clearing where the penumbra of an almost-given will be able to enter and modify its contour.*[13]

But "receive" from where? Who or what is sending? What is the source of the "penumbra of an almost-given"? We have already provided the answer. The voices are there in the subtle modifications of a trillion synapses knit together into the feltwork of the brain. From there we receive the strong associations that lead us along like Ariadne's thread, or the quiet, almost inaudible ones that take us aside into rooms we did not know existed.

Clearly, for this process to work, a richly structured store of memories and associations is necessary. But another feature, involving its organization, enables the brain to select. Unlike any machine we know, the brain operates on mechanisms that span an enormous range of physical scales. This is true of living tissue in general. It has been pointed out that a misplaced group of atoms in a single molecule can kill an elephant. Niels Bohr speaks of "the peculiar organization in which features that may be analyzed by usual mechanics are interwoven with typically atomistic features to an extent unparalleled in inanimate matter.''[14]

Thus, while in machines the microworld of thermal noise and quantum uncertainty are far removed in scale from the *macroscopic* operations of pistons, levers, and springs, no such sharp separation exists in the brain. We must assume that minute fluctuations can percolate upward and become expressed as such macroscopic features as the action potentials of nerve cells. If this is true, then all the uncertainties and unpredictabilities of the microworld can make their way into our thoughts and our actions.[15]

This is sometimes called *bottom-up* control: events on a small scale determine events on a larger scale. The forces between water molecules determine the property of liquidity of bulk water. Polanyi[16] pointed out that the opposite, *top-down* control, is rare in inanimate nature but common in living systems. An example is the detailed structure of the DNA molecule, which is the product of eons of evolution of species. Thus the world of atoms and the macroscopic world of human behavior are linked by both bottom-up and top-down control.

How far down into the microworld does this connectedness reach? From what depths are we able to fetch our thoughts? What minuscule cerebral events can become the sources of our inventiveness, our creativity, our fancy? I believe there is no limit.

In chapter 10, I discussed the physical phenomenon of *chaos*. These are processes characterized—among other things—by *nonlinearity*, a term that refers to mathematical properties relating the different variables in a physical process.[17] It can be stated that linear processes are generally easy to understand, and their outcomes are predictable. Nonlinear processes are notoriously difficult to treat and frequently are chaotic. Recall that in chaotic systems the path the system takes depends so critically on some of the variables that the minutest change quickly becomes amplified and will totally change the outcome. Chaotic systems not only are unpredictable, as are most nonlinear systems, but also are sensitive to fluctuations that are ever-present in any physical system but too small to be sensed and taken into account by an observer.

I propose that neural dynamics is chaotic in the sense described. This does not mean that thinking is a meaningless jumble, only that there is no known limit to the smallness of events that can trigger a sequence of thoughts, determine the trajectory of the Joycean stream of consciousness.

But if such chance fluctuations as atomistic noise and perhaps quantum uncertainty can determine what we think, they also determine what we do. Can *chance* be enlisted to explain free will?

It is often stated that since we have no control over the vagaries of chance, no personal freedom can be gained from this. "Chance cannot be directional" is the way the English neurophysiologist J. Z. Young expressed it.

The noisy background of course has no will, no direction. It merely provides a rich source of seeds from which we can select and which we can let grow or discard. Freeman Dyson hints at this when he says that "free will is the coupling of a human mind to otherwise random processes inside the brain."[10]

Dyson's statement may derive from a religious conviction. He leaves open the question of how this coupling of mind and chance takes place. I believe we are dealing here with the most subtle of processes that exist in nature. Somehow, the top-down control that is so characteristic of living systems must exert its selective power over the myriad microscopic potentialities dredged up by the chaotic dynamics. The selection of these chance events and their elaboration through countless creative loops is the function of consciousness, which is like a wedge that is interposed between causal past and ordained future.

There still remains the mystery of the subjective *feeling* of being conscious. Quite clearly, some very novel and unique property has crept into the neural works. But strange and awesome things happen in the nonlinear world, such as bootstrap processes in which something appears to arise out of nothing. Totally new phenomena may occur. An amplifier connected to a microphone and loudspeaker may suddenly produce an earsplitting wail. Perhaps a minute fluctuation in the amplifier produced a faint sound in the speaker which is picked up by the microphone and then amplified to produce a louder sound on the speaker. The loop rapidly builds up the sound until the microphone or the amplifier or the loudspeaker becomes saturated.

For small amounts of the element uranium 235, the amount of radiation emitted rises smoothly with the amount of the material. But beyond a certain *critical mass*, nuclear fission processes become self-sustaining, and we have a nuclear chain reaction. If we could isolate a piece of uranium 235 of greater than critical mass and then allow a single neutron to enter the chunk, it would result in an atomic bomb explosion. This can be explained by the iterative or self-referent character of the process: the number of neutrons produced in the chunk depends on the level of neutrons present, which depends on the number of neutrons produced.

Nonlinearity combined with self-reference has produced unexpected and utterly astounding results in pure mathematics. In ordinary geometry we define figures in two, three, or more dimensions by simple arithmetic statements, equations. There is one equation defining a circle, another for an ellipse, others for spheres, ellipsoids, and so on. But when one goes from such simple expressions to statements that are self-referent, patterns appear that leave you breathless. These can be computed and shown on the monitor screen of any desktop computer by entering a program that is a simple *loop* of instructions.[19] The results are not ordinary shapes with defined boundaries.

The most famous of these, the *Mandelbrot set*, is a *structure*—I don't know what else to call it—of almost haunting beauty. But its strangeness goes far beyond its visual appeal. The Mandelbrot set is a structure of truly *infinite* detail. Any small portion of it can be amplified, revealing more detail and new forms. James Gleick, in his book *Chaos*, describes this feature as follows:

> *If the set were thought of as a planet-sized object, a personal computer could show the whole object, or features the size of cities, or the size of buildings, or the size of rooms, or the size of books, or the size of letters, or the size of bacteria, or the size of atoms. The people who looked at such pictures saw that all the scales had similar patterns, yet every scale was different. And all these microscopic landscapes were generated by the same few lines of computer code.*[20]

Why this digression to Mandelbrot sets? I suggest that there is more than a circumstantial analogy between these nonlinear self-referent structures and the operation of the brain, which is also nonlinear and self-referent. The resulting structures, our thoughts, don't have defined boundaries. They are not *of* one particular object or event, but a little bit of this and a little bit of that, shimmering structures with built-in zoomability. Consciousness is perhaps just another of the strange phenomena that populate this nonlinear world.

Chapter 14

Man and Machine: Homo ex Machina?

I have been presenting a physicalist model of mind-brain interaction. It has not introduced any process or agency that invalidates physical laws as presently understood. On the contrary, it has used contemporary physics to free brain mechanisms from the materialistic constraints of older theories.

It still leaves open the question whether mental phenomena could be produced by means other than natural, biological brains. Are our creative animations, culminating in the universal machine of the computer, capable of acquiring not just purpose and function but also the ability to think and feel?

The computer metaphor of the mind-brain is a powerful argument here because of the computer's own dual aspect. Its software often is cited as the analog of the immaterial ingredient that causes brains to have minds. By thus mystifying the computer, we have demystified the brain. We have arrived at a kind of materialist dualism.

But if we look more closely at the software, we find that it is only a presciption for setting switches that determine what the computer is to do under different circumstances. Software specifies that the hardware should do X if it encounters the situation A, otherwise do Y. The instruction may be more complex: If A and B, but not C, then do X; otherwise do Y. If this sounds too deterministic, we can even throw in some uncertainty: "If A and B but not C, then throw dice and if they show *seven* do X; otherwise do Y." (The throw of the dice, of course, can be simulated by the computer, which is—remember—a universal machine.)

I argued in chapter 12 that there probably are serious obstacles to the idea of transferring an individual's consciousness onto a machine, the *downloading* of knowledge base onto an all-purpose artificial brain. This does not preclude the possibility of a non-neural "brain" being led through its own "lifetime" of experience, after which it may lead an intelligent, and perhaps even conscious, existence.

If so, then we also must admit the possibility of superior performance by the artificial brain and contemplate our own future obsolecence. Somebody recently calculated that by the year 2025 the human brain will have reached its limits for absorbing facts and figures. The knowledge explosion that began in earnest in the present century will have saturated our neural memory banks. Among the many dire predictions for mankind's future, this is perhaps the saddest: no more intellectual progress. No further expansion of human knowledge. Stagnation.

But there may be a glimmer of hope. Even if we are doomed, perhaps our creations can carry on. There will soon be—we are told— a race of super-intelligent supercomputing robots, capable of handling their gigabyte memories with gigaflop nimbleness. (A *gigabyte* is a memory store that can accommodate a billion letters of the alphabet, and a *gigaflop* is a processing speed of a billion elementary operations per second.) Our best hope is that the robots will be benevolent, or—as Nabokov put it even before the dawn of the computer age—that "the good of mankind was so contagious that it infected metal." If we are lucky, they may keep us around as pets.

The brain, it is true, has its computational limitations, and the above scenario is not too farfetched if we assume—as is the fashion nowadays—that it is the brain's main function to compute. I will come back soon to examine this proposition. But what about the prediction of the end of our intellectual reach by 2025?

We will probably have to go back beyond the Stone Age to encounter a situation where all knowledge was contained in the portable memory banks in the head. With the advent of language, the individual had gained access to the information carried by his or her entire tribe. The invention of the written word provided an enormously expanded data base. Already in antiquity, the library had become indispensable to progress.

Today, even routine tasks are unthinkable without frequent consultation of written instructions, and no cultural endeavor could proceed without the aid of extensive information stored on written page or magnetic disk. With the arrival of the electronic computer about midcentury, another dimension was added to our cognitive dependence. Not only the tabulation of facts but their categorization and analysis were being carried out external to our brains. The modern computer is able to draw conclusions, make predictions, evaluate massive data at speeds the unaided brain could never hope to achieve.

We are wedded to this technology notwithstanding laments about the depersonalization of our lives. The problem of public health is a case in point. In the United States, the Centers for Disease Control, located in Atlanta, Georgia, is a high-tech establishment in which enormous quantities of data pertaining to the health of the nation are continually tabulated, sorted, sifted, and analyzed by high-speed computers. Local environmental factors affecting health are detected in this way, illnesses are traced to new products that have appeared on the market, and outbreaks of communicable diseases are spotted early and tracked to their sources.

Is it unreasonable to predict that by 2025 we will have reached the end of our intellectual tether? Is it not apparent that machine intelligence is outwitting its human creators? Is it so farfetched to expect intelligent machines to take over when the human drama has played out?

The problem of machine intelligence is far more than a question of the cleverness of our gadgetry. It goes to the core of our own existence and significance. It is the mirror in which we search for our uniqueness.

Magic Trick

Allow me now to perform a little thought experiment. In the 1930s the neuroanatomist Karl Lashley chipped away at rats' brains in a vain attempt to find the location of memory. It seemed to be everywhere and nowhere. I will do something similar with you as the subject. Don't be alarmed. Nothing essential will be removed, and anyway, it is only make-believe.

The block diagram below represents *you* (the big box) communicating with the outside world. The contacts go both ways: from the outside world through a smaller box labeled *S*, for *sensory systems*, and on to the *higher brain centers* (*HBC*). It is the function of that box to generate your appropriate responses to the sensory messages and to convey these responses via the *motor system (M)* back to the outside world.

We now perform the first operation, a cut along the dotted line, eliminating the motor system and all contact with the outside world. This may sound drastic, but I will replace the motor system with a very sophisticated computer that can simulate the outside world and send all the appropriate signals to your sensory system. In a sense, your brain already does this when you dream.

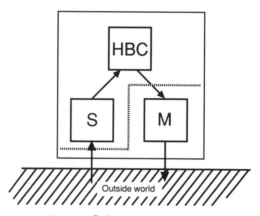

The big box represents you. S *is your sensory system,* M *your motor system, and* HBC *your higher brain centers.*

Our computer will do better. Higher realism. No nightmares. In fact, I can promise you a life that will be as pleasant and successful as anything you ever dreamed of. I will call this computer the *pseudo-world* (PW) because it presents your sensory system with all the stimuli of a real world. Also, your higher brain centers can react back on it as though a motor system were reaching out and contacting a real world. You do that in your dreams also, without moving a muscle, and new computer programs can interact similarly with both your senses and muscles, creating what is called *virtual reality.* What I am proposing is a complete and permanent virtual reality. We now have all of you and your world contained in a neat little box, your own private cyberspace.

The second operation is a minor one. Your higher brain centers, being a kind of neural machine, react to all stimuli in what is, in principle, a predictable way. Thus, if *PW* simulates your participating in a game of tennis, it will generate the sights, sounds, and feel of all action and convey them to *S*. It also can be made to include your own reactions to what is going on. Since my supercomputer in *PW* no longer needs the instructions from *HBC*, we can eliminate the connections from *HBC* to *PW* (cut along dotted line).

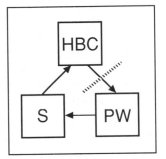

You, *after the first surgery.*

The next step follows logically. The higher brain centers now are redundant, since it was their function to generate the responses. These are now computed in the *PW* and sent to the sensory system. The *HBC* now can be removed without loss.

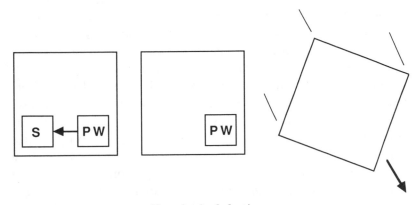

Your logical destiny.

With the higher brain centers gone, the sensory system no longer serves a function. We can remove it with impunity.

With the last step, our pseudo-world computer *PW* has lost its audience. We will turn it off, remove it, and throw away the empty box that was *you*.

As I told you, nothing essential was taken from you. Or have I overlooked something?

Does the Brain Compute?

The so-called *computational approach* to brain function was pioneered by the school of *cognitive science*, a cross between psychology and artificial intelligence. It states quite simply that for the brain to arrive at any kind of understanding, whether the recognition of a face or the proof of a mathematical theorem, it must go through a series of simple logical steps. Any kind of brain function, so the story goes, in principle can be broken down into sequences of such primitive operations. Hence any brain function can, by the same principle, be carried out by a computer. The brain is, in fact, a computer, and the neuroscientist's task is to find the logical steps that constitute intelligent behavior. Having done so, he or she also will have laid the foundation for constructing an equally intelligent machine.

We must understand here that, when we speak of *intelligent machines*, we might as well talk of computers. The modern electronic digital computer not only is the most advanced piece of machinery, but is in a true sense *every* machine we have ever built. The same hardware can compute the position of the planet Pluto ten thousand years from now, run a factory, do your income tax, and predict the behavior of an experimental airfoil at supersonic speeds. It can predict the dynamics of any process that we can specify, simulate any machine, actual or contemplated.

Let us consider the computers at the Centers for Disease Control, mentioned above. As an example, assume that scattered cases of a new form of severe allergy have appeared in a part of the country where a new chemical plant recently began operating. Also, certain new pharmaceuticals just appeared on the market in the same region. Statistical tests, however, point to yet another likely source of the problem: farms in the area recently have begun to use a new type of chemical fertilizer. From the available data, the computers are unable to assign the cause of the allergies to any one of these events with absolute certainty.

At this point a few of the scientists get together and *think*. Should they close down the chemical plant? Do they have enough evidence to justify that? Should they take the new pharmaceuticals off the market? Or ban the new fertilizer? Run some tests?

What are the pros and cons involved in all these decisions, and why can't the computers run through all the possible scenarios and pick the best one? Perhaps they could, but what do we mean by the *best*? We quickly realize that some of the considerations are extremely difficult to express as simple logical steps. Each alternative involves questionable gains and probable damage to some sector of the population. There will be criticisms. Some people will fight back. The issue may become political. Perhaps the severity of the allergies had been exaggerated. Also, the numbers are small. Perhaps it is best to do nothing and wait. But then, what if some of the victims should die?

We recall again Dennett's assertion that thinking is but the combined action of many homunculi, each carrying out primitive logical steps. A task may seem hopelessly complex, such as the above problem of deciding what to do about the allergy outbreak. Dennett's prescription is to subdivide such tasks into more and more primitive *boxes* of elementary tasks, to be accomplished by smaller, more stupid homunculi.

> *Eventually this nesting of boxes within boxes lands you with homunculi so stupid (all they have to do is remember whether to say yes or no when asked) that they can be, as one says, "replaced by a machine." One* discharges *fancy homunculi from one's scheme by organizing armies of such idiots to do the work.*[1]

Not everyone believes that this recipe will work in all cases. Howard Gardner, a cognitive scientist at Harvard and a strong advocate of the computer metaphor of the brain, argues in the end that we are facing what he calls a *computational paradox*, which is the breakdown of the computer analogy. He points out that computer models may be adequate for some brain functions, such as visual perception. Referring to these, he writes that

> *the kinds of descriptions that are legitimately offered in the terms of a digital von Neumann computer may turn out to be appropriate accounts of these human cognitive processes. . . . But as one moves to more complex and belief-tainted processes. . .or judgments concerning rival courses of action, the computational model becomes less adequate. Human beings apparently do not approach these tasks in a manner that can be characterized as logical or rational or that entail step-by-step symbolic processing. Rather, they employ*

> *heuristics, strategies, biases, images, and other vague and approximate approaches. The kinds of symbol-manipulation models invoked by Newell, Simon, and others in the first generation of cognitivists do not seem optimal for describing such central human capacities. . . . Human thought emerges as messy, intuitive, subject to subjective representations—not as pure and immaculate calculations.*[2]

It may be argued at this point that the "messy, intuitive" part of our thinking has more to do with our intellectual limitations than with any presumed advantage we have over the computer. To return to the example of the allergy outbreak, is it not true that the ramifications of any of the alternative choices are just too vast and unpredictable for us to select by logical rules? And isn't it the same shortcoming that prevents us from programming the computer to supply the answer? But a choice has to be made, and so we rely on our "messy" intuitions. That they are not the high road to truth has been demonstrated by the countless wrong choices we have made in the past.

But Gardner has a point. The "messy, intuitive" part of our thinking does more than just guess where logic leaves us stranded. It is responsible for all the creative leaps the human mind is capable of, and it still writes the only sonnets worth reading.

I believe that there is another, more profound reason why the computer metaphor of the brain is flawed. It has to do with the fact that, unlike the brain, the computer must have a client who imposes on it a code and a set of logical and semantic rules. Somebody presents it with a problem and somebody takes cognizance of the results. Sometimes, instead of some*body*, there is some*thing*, a machine or system that is controlled and has its needs attended to by a computer. This *supersystem* again follows the dictates of a human creator. In isolation the computer would be a useless contraption, its workings devoid of meaning.

The computer has to be in communication with its client. We must devise codes for translating our language into strings of zeros and ones (called a *computer language*) and back again into our language. The computer is a fast and reliable manipulator and executor of algorithms involving symbols. Thus a string of zeros and ones (really two different states of magnetization on a tape or disk) may stand for the number 22.5, and another string for the number 7.2. Yet another may be the command "*multiply.*" On receipt, the machine will carry out a number of operations causing another string of zeros and ones to appear at a certain register. After a decoding process that is the inverse of the coding rules that defined the original two symbols, the new one translates into the number 162. We say that the computer has carried out the multiplication of 22.5 and 7.2 and produced the correct answer, 162.

It hasn't. *We* did the multiplying. Instead of pencil and paper or a slide rule, we used a computer. It doesn't know numbers, it knows only states of magnetization on its various components. In fact, it doesn't really *know* anything. It simply *is* what we built and *does* what it is told. This is true for the simple example given above as well as for the most sophisticated program we feed into it.

It will be objected that my example of the multiplication of 22.5 and 7.2 is more a task for a cheap hand calculator and is an insult to the intelligence of a computer running on sophisticated software. Once we have loaded a program containing perhaps many thousands of instructions into its memory, provided it with a rich set of data, and given it the command to *run*, we have no way of knowing what profound truths it will reveal, what unexpected treasure of knowledge it will lead us to—or what reams of utter nonsense, if we made a single mistake in one of the thousands of instructions.

Between our instructions and the final results there is a never-never land of hidden logic, of unfathomable electronic mastications, of billions of zeros changed into ones and ones back again into zeros. And yet every single one of these microscopic events follows logically and inevitably from those preceding.

How do we know? The computer does exactly what human designers meant it to do. This does not mean that any one person can follow all the details of its operation. Electronic engineers designed the elementary storage and logic units, the *chips*. Computer engineers put together an *architecture* from thousands of these building blocks. Software engineers wrote elaborate internal languages and codes so that the *programmer* can easily express his or her particular problems in an instruction set called the *program*.

It is this opaqueness of the workings of the machine, stemming from its enormous complexity, that invites speculation of human attributes, of autonomous thought, of purposive behavior. I am trying to show here that—this opaqueness notwithstanding—the thoughts and the purposes are ours, not the machine's. Beyond all the fanfare and mystique we have woven around it, the accomplishments of the computer are a tribute to *our* intelligence, not to that of the machine.

The story has been told recently of a sophisticated pattern recognition device scientists had developed for the U.S. Army. It was an artificial neural network like the perceptron shown on page 55. The net was *trained* to detect the presence of tanks in a landscape. The training consisted in showing the device many photographs of scenes, some with tanks, some without. In some cases—as in the picture on page 143—the tank's presence was not very obvious. The inputs to the neural net were digitized photographs; the outputs were just two possible states that were arbitrarily labeled "*tank*" and "*no tank*." In the training phase, when a picture containing a tank was shown, and when the output "*tank*" appeared, the network was rewarded by reinforcing certain connections between the artificial neurons. The same procedure applied when a "*no tank*" picture was accompanied by a "*no tank*" output. But when an "*incorrect*" output appeared, other changes were made according to prescribed rules.

After a great many learning trials it was found that the network outputs were nearly 100 percent "correct." The network was able to detect tanks in the landscape even if they were barely noticeable. Or so it appeared.

A new set of photographs was produced to confirm the intelligence of the device. But this time it failed dismally, performing no better than chance.

It took some soul-searching before the mystery was cleared up. The neural net did learn to make a distinction, but it had nothing to do with tanks. It so happened that in the first series all the photographs with tanks were taken on a sunny day; those without tanks, on a cloudy day (it may have been the other way round). The outputs did not mean "*tank*" and "*no tank*," but had a high correlation with "*clouds*" and "*no clouds*."

I mention this example not to poke fun at AI, but to point up the subtle difficulties in the use of codes between man and machine and the danger in assigning meaning to output states of a machine. Note also that in the recognition scheme that the brain uses according to my theory of perception (pages 143–144), no such misreading of the code can occur.

We return again to the original question: Is the brain like a computer? In some respects, yes. Like the computer, it has a *client*: the body that it guides and whose needs it attends to. But beyond its many chores, its housekeeping functions—and while it is doing these—it is engaged in extensive leisure activity. It reminisces, plans, daydreams, *thinks*. No internal code is required for that, because the brain speaks to itself. It is its own client. No misunderstanding is possible. To say that "the brain computes," apart from pointing to some all too obvious analogies, carries little meaning. It is like saying that "a telescope computes the trajectory of light rays passing through it."[3]

The Turing Test

We spoke of intelligent machines, also called "machines that think," as though there were general agreement on the meaning of thought and intelligence. The mirror image to our question "Does the brain compute?" is "Can machines think?" This question was raised in just this form more than forty years ago by the young English mathematician Alan Turing. He also supplied the answer: *yes*, providing the machine could pass a certain test that has become known as the Turing Test.[4] It has remained at the heart of the continuing controversy regarding machine intelligence.

Turing managed to circumvent the question of what constitutes thought or intelligence. He did this by asserting that a machine possesses both if, on being quizzed, its answers cannot be distinguished from that of a human. Since humans think—whatever thinking means—to be indistinguishable from a human is to be capable of thought.

And so Turing proposed the *imitation game*. An interrogator communicates with a machine that is located in a different room and tries to decide whether he or she is talking to another human or to a machine. The answers are designed to trick the interrogator into believing they come from a human. To the extent that this deception works, Turing suggests, the machine must be accorded intelligence.

Turing quotes the following passage from a *Lister oration* presented by G. Jefferson:

> *Not until a machine can write*
> *a sonnet or compose a concerto because of thoughts and emotions*
> *felt, and not by the chance fall of symbols, could we agree that*
> *machine equals brain—that is, not only write it but know that*
> *it had written it. No mechanism could feel (and not merely arti-*
> *ficially signal, an easy contrivance) pleasure at its success, grief*

*when its valves fuse, be warmed by flattery, be made miserable
by its mistakes, be charmed by sex, be angry or depressed when
it cannot get what it wants.*

Turing then attempts to refute Jefferson by pointing out that
there is no way of knowing if (and what) the machine thinks, unless one could *be* that machine—which is no different from knowing that another person thinks. If you doubt one, you should doubt
the other. It is known as the *solipsist* point of view.

One could raise many objections to the validity of the Turing
Test. It is never stated, for example, how long or extensive the
questioning should be, or how intelligent a person the machine
is supposed to imitate. With a few grunts and "I dunno's," it could
easily mimic a moron. This was the strategy of Spallanzani's beau-
tiful puppet, introduced in chapter 4. On the other hand, suspi-
cions would be raised if it acts too smart. When asked "What is
the cuberoot of 15,625?"—something the most primitive hand calculator can do in a flash—it had better pretend it does not know
the answer. Thus, to prove its intelligence, it must act dumb.

But the main difficulty comes from Turing's insistence that
the performance of a task is tantamount to consciousness of the
task. We have seen the fallacy of that assumption in connection
with the phenomenon of blindsight. Certain damage to parts of
the nervous system causes a person to lose conscious perception
of sight but allows him nevertheless to perform as though he saw
(see discussion in chapter 13). We are not justified, therefore, in
the assumption that performance implies *conscious* performance.
And since we don't yet understand what neural mechanisms are
missing in blindsight, it is a farfetched assumption that we had
inadvertently built these into our machine.

It is true, of course, that we *know* only of our own thoughts,
and can only *attribute* thinking and consciousness to other people.
Such attribution, as I have pointed out, is a voluntary act. We could
be solipsists if we wanted to be. To make the attribution of consciousness is, however, an act based on the knowledge of a profound kinship that exists between all humans, our commonness
of descent at the end of a three-billion-year-long evolution, our
equal biological needs and wants, and the fundamental similarity
of our instruments of thought, our brains. All these factors give
me a sense of solidarity with the human race and induce me to
believe that the poet who wrote the sonnet knows that he or she

wrote it and feels pleasure at its success. I do not feel obligated to extend the same attribution to the sonnet-writing computer, or to feel sympathy for a machine. They are just not our kind!

If being able to carry out arithmetic operations at lightning speed is to be called *intelligent*, then computers certainly are intelligent, and if searching memory banks and drawing logical conclusions is called *thinking*, then computers certainly are thinking machines, although I have the reservation, mentioned before, that—in the last analysis—it is the human behind the machine who is really doing the thinking.

We must remind ourselves, also, that computers are not the first machines to which such human attributes have been assigned. We mentioned the clockworks that thrilled audiences in eighteenth-century France. It was always the cutting edge of technology that was regarded with breathless awe not only by the man in the street, but also by the creators of that technology. Today the high-speed electronic computer is endowed by us with a mystique we would not accord a mechanical machine of gears and levers, no matter how complicated. But in 1832, when Charles Babbage in England invented a mechanical calculator, a contemporary wrote that "the wondrous pulp and fibre of the brain has been substituted by brass and iron; he (Babbage) has taught wheelwork to think."[5]

But the advocates of the orthodox materialist interpretation of human thought, and of what is known as *hard AI*, are not satisfied with just having their computers think. They insist that machines also *feel*, or at least have the capacity to feel. It hasn't happened yet, but sooner or later one of the promoters of artificial intelligence will use the term *racist* to describe somebody who doubts that machines can have feelings, and they will invoke the Turing Test to back up their argument.

How Do *We* Think?

Brains, we decided, do some computing when they think, and computers appear to think, if searching for answers is considered thinking. Machines thus are capable of some form of intelligence— we call it *AI*, and humans often exhibit machinelike qualities, which I have dubbed the *indigenous android* (*IA*). Is there then no fundamental difference between us and our creations, between the puppet and the puppeteer?

Is our thinking fundamentally the same as that of the computer? How do *we* think?

As I search for an answer, I hear no chorus of a thousand dimwits, no busy chatter between tribes of homunculi. In fact, at first there is an embarrassing silence. Ah. Thinking! Yes. Let's see now. What happens when I think? I must think of something. What? Anything.

What did I do today? Worked in the garden. Tomatoes about to bloom. Rabbit nibbled off the tops of my basil. There he sat munching away at the tender shoots, one-eyeing me from the side. Damn rabbit! I am against hunting, but what can I do? Catch him in a box and take him somewhere else? Why do I say *him*? It may be a lady rabbit, Ms. Rabbit. Miserable rabbit.

This isn't telling me anything I didn't know. There is awareness to my thoughts and selectivity, exclusivity, chaining, and unitarity to my awareness (see pages 138–144). I can make a computer imitate most of these attributes. What is puzzling is the problem of how my mind unerringly relates the brain's internal activity to the physical reality outside, unlike the AI tank detector I described before. How do certain events that happen in my brain now relate to the rabbit I saw a few hours ago? Locke long ago postulated that there must be a certain resemblance between real objects and their mental representations that allows us to make the connection, a view known as *naive realism.* My own picture of images generated peripherally by more central brain areas is, in a sense, a return to Locke's naive realism.

The awareness itself is the big stumbling block. Perhaps, if I really understood the underlying brain mechanisms, I would understand what the computer is lacking. I already discussed the psychoneural identity theory (see page 100). To say that a thought is a sequence of particular neural states is an empty statement. But we can still choose from a large menu of *isms.* There is *substance dualism, property dualism, functionalism, logical empiricism, epiphenomenalism,* the already mentioned *naive realism,* and, of course, the computer metaphor.[6]

Among the above, functionalism is perhaps the current favorite. According to that philosophy, the particular system that does the thinking—in our case, the human brain—is irrelevant. Its functioning could be replaced by any number of equivalent hardware, not necessarily composed of neurons. It matters only that given causes produce given results—that certain *behavior* follow certain inputs to the brain. If another mechanism functions the same way, then it is equivalent to a brain. *It* feels, if we can say that the brain feels. *It* thinks, if we can say that the brain thinks.

Clearly, functionalism leaves open the possibility of artificial—that is, man-made—intelligence. In a wider sense, it also means that *life* need not be based on carbon chemistry, but could be constructed—and might even evolve naturally—into forms based on entirely different principles. Some of the boldest fantasies were envisioned by the theoretical physicist Freeman Dyson, who speaks of structures of cosmic dimensions appropriate to a future, vastly expanded universe. His predictions are truly heroic in scope, looking ahead not millions or billions of years, but 10^{33} (a trillion trillion billion) years. At that time, matter as we now know it may have ceased to exist, the protons and neutrons that make up the nuclei of our atoms having all turned into radiation. But life may overcome even that formidable barrier. Given the immense stretches of time and the imperceptibly slow changes in the nature of the cosmos, life very well may evolve into forms that seem utterly fantastic to us now but are just adaptations to a new world. Dyson's vision is thus realistic, given his faith in the primacy of life in the universe. He is unwilling to contemplate a lifeless world, ever. Borrowing a line from Shakespeare's *Twelfth Night*, he characterizes this faith as "whispers of immortality."[7]

Dyson thinks of these bizarre structures that span unimaginable distances as the biological heirs to present-day life forms, having all of our attributes of consciousness and intelligence, perhaps in prodigiously expanded form. It is functionalism on a grandiose scale. The visions are fantastic but conceivable. It is, I think, less plausible that a machine conceived today on the basis of our incomplete understanding of what constitutes our mind should exhibit those properties we understand the least.

Whether or not machines may offer us hope to ride out the distant future, some immediate problems loom large, at least in the minds of some contemporary commentators. We have, according to them, entered an epoch in which our celebrated minds have turned stagnant. Dyson's dream of an eternal destiny may be cut short, not by the bang of nuclear insanity—it looks as though we may have avoided that fate at least for now—but by the whimper of our dying minds, an exhaustion of our ingenuity, the end of our imagination. It is not the supposed exhaustion of our cerebral memory banks, which was predicted for the year 2025, but a dearth of new material to put into them. What we hear on this score is not mere whispers but a loud and persuasive chorus of voices, all proclaiming that our time of glory may be at an end.

Chapter 15

The Measure of All Things
or
"Don't Copy That Floppy"

The doomsayers belong to a school referred to broadly as postmodernism. They are different from the millennialists of yore who also predicted the end of civilization, but who at least held out the hope of paradise for some of us. This new doom is absolute and final.

Let us hear some of these voices. "This is no ordinary time," announces the 1986 Post-Modern Manifesto. "The modern age opened with the destruction of God and religion. It is ending with the threatened destruction of all coherent thought. The age was held on course by stories of progress and emancipation. . . . But these stories are now exhausted. There are no new stories to replace them. . .disillusion has lurked in the wings of European culture for two centuries. Now it can command center stage. We are paralyzed by the performance and we cannot leave the theater. All the exits are blocked."[1]

Postmodernist writers speak of the end of history, the end of art, the end of man. What does all this mean? Why this bleak forecast?

The proclaimed death of man seems closely tied to a literary dilemma, or at least a perceived literary dilemma, called the end of the narrative. It is held that every story has been told, every linguistic trick exploited, and so we wind up with the *un*story of

165

Thomas Pynchon's *V,* an antinovel whose antihero is called, significantly, Herbert Stencil. Since narrative has come to an end, we also can no longer tell the story of man, who seems to be reduced to reliving millennia-old archetypes. Sophocles knew us as well as any modern writer, and we can't flush old Oedipus out of our system. The French postmodernist writer Jean-François Lyotard describes "thinking as disaster, nomadism, difference and redundancy. Let us write our graffiti," he laments, "since we can't engrave."[2]

Everything sayable has been said. "Creating the new," Kearney points out, "means choosing from the old." Paraphrasing Derrida, he calls imagination, which has been the fuel of progress since the beginning of civilization, "a mass-produced postcard addressed 'to whom it may concern' and wandering aimlessly through a communications network, devoid of 'destiny' or 'destination.' "[3]

Umberto Eco, the Italian writer known for his novel *The Name of the Rose*, has given us a somber account of this postmodern dilemma in his *Travels in Hyperreality* (1986). Hyperreality is the perfect image, the most authentic imitation, the ultimate fake. He sees it in the hodgepodge of fakes crammed into the Hearst Castle in Los Angeles, in the ultrarealistic displays of Disneyland, where sophisticated techniques called *audio-animatronics* create the perfect illusion of life. "Disney's robots are masterpieces of electronics; each was devised by observing the expressions of a real actor, then building models, then developing skeletons of absolute precision, authentic computers in human form to be dressed in 'flesh' and 'skin' made by craftsmen whose command of realism is incredible."

The perfect fake must transcend reality:

> *A real crocodile can be found in the zoo, and as a rule it is dozing or hiding, but Disneyland tells us that faked nature corresponds much more to our daydream demands. When, in the space of twenty-four hours, you go (as I did deliberately) from the fake New Orleans of Disneyland to the real one, and from the wild river of Adventureland to a trip on the Mississippi where the captain of the paddle-wheel steamer says it is possible to see alligators on the banks of the river, and then you don't see any, you risk feeling homesick for Disneyland, where the wild animals don't have to be coaxed.[4]*

Eco saves his most stinging remarks for the Palace of Living Arts in Buena Vista, Los Angeles. Here, "the great masterpieces of painting and sculpture of all time" are rendered as full-color, life-size, and lifelike wax figures shown next to photographs of their pallid, time-ravaged originals. Kearney, echoing Eco's sentiments, writes in a chapter titled "Post-Modern Culture: Apocalypse Now?":

> *But the crowning exhibit of the Palace's entire collection is, undoubtedly, the* Venus de Milo. *There we see her in all her pristine splendour, leaning gracefully against an Ionian column of a classical temple with both arms now intact and her life-like colouring and gestures fully restored! Just as the original model would have stood before the original classical artist. As the accompanying inscription boasts: "Here is Venus de Milo brought to life as she was in the time when she posed for the unknown sculptor in Greece some two hundred years B.C." And to highlight the claim that this reconstruction, made possible by the most advanced techniques of laser reproduction and holography, is far more "real" than the art-work it imitates, we are also presented with a small but exact copy of the one-armed, lustre-less and time-worn statue as it appears in the Louvre of Paris. Make no mistake about it, The Palace of Living Arts proclaims, the life-like reconstruction before your eyes is far more authentic than the classical original.*[5]

We may be tempted to dismiss the phenomena of Disneyland, Hearst's Castle, and the Palace of Living Arts as just local concentrations of kitsch, and Eco's and Kearney's comments as a bit of California-bashing.

Imitation, as I have said, is the source of imagination and creativity. Is it that our imitations have become so perfect that they leave no more room for imagination?

I remember, as a child growing up in Vienna, the fantasy world of the Prater with its clumsy imitations that seemed to be endless sources of imagination. There was a *Train to Venice*. It consisted of a single car that stood immobile on a short section of track. But the simulated noises of the puffing engine, the calling of the stations, the whistles, the clattering wheels, and the painted scenery being drawn slowly past the windows, were enough to make me want to go back again and again. That fake train ride had left me with an unquenchable desire for traveling that is still with me today.

What, then, is the trouble with today's hyperrealities? Have the postmodernist writers perhaps forgotten their childhood? Are their criticisms too sweeping, too pessimistic? The man in the street, more concerned with the state of the economy, is largely unaware of postmodernist gloom. And all over the world many more people are dying from lack of food than from lack of ideas.

But the themes of imagination turned stale, of images becoming hyperreality, of art becoming anti-art, even of science reaching the end of its tether, pervade much of contemporary human culture.

At the core of these complaints seems to be our facile and sterile imitation of everything around us, including our own works. There is a dearth of new ideas. They are deemed unnecessary. Postmodern architecture is a collage of existing and past styles with no pretense of anything new having been added.

Imitation is driven by a sophisticated technology of duplication and dissemination. One of the early advertisements for Xerox photocopiers showed a secretary who, after making copies of a letter, did not know which was the original. We live in an age of the facsimile, the *simulacrum*.

How did we get here, and what are we to do?

Humanity started the career of building a culture by being imitators. "The pleasure of imitation," says Eco, "as the ancients knew, is one of the most innate in the human spirit."[6] We imitate reality, first only by producing mental images, pictures-in-the-head, nebulous structures that in their fleeting existence are able to spawn more images. When man learned to externalize images and place them alongside reality, he had taken a giant step. The great paleolithic cave paintings are mental images stored in pigment, thoughts frozen into stone so they can be recalled at will and reexamined.

The significance of this step lies in the fact that we have succeeded in reversing the transition from object to image. We have objectified the mental image, and we are now able to form images of it. We attach gravity to it, literally and figuratively. It may become an object of veneration and acquire in our minds functions and powers far beyond its intrinsically imitative origin. Imagination creates objects of imitation, and imitation carries imagination beyond its original intent. The child's toy, the religious icon, the voodoo doll.

The objectification of images has taken two distinct and complementary paths. In one, the product becomes an object of contemplation, a work of art, a theory about nature or man, a piece of music. In the other, imagination conceives, and our hands fashion, objects of use, tools and, eventually, machines. In all of these endeavors the human has been the originator and chief recipient.

Humanism rests on the twin pillars of arts and science, on the one hand, and technology on the other. Both have their roots in our imagination and are propelled by our urge to imitate.

But now we are told that imagination is dead and imitation is running on empty. This has produced, in Kearney's words, a hall-of-mirrors effect, a "vicious spiral of reflexivity."[7] Artists seem to be frantically searching for some yet undiscovered means of expression, creative minds for something to create, writers to keep alive the narrative, while copies of past achievements are flooding our culture by the millions, and the vapid tunes of Muzak follow us from the shopping mall to the dentist's chair. We have entered the doldrums, and the sails of our imagination are slack.

"The machines will get better—more like humans perhaps—while, at the same time, humans may well become more like machines. The paths are convergent," predicts O. B. Hardison.[8] Think again of the wonders of Disney's audio-animatronics. At the same time, on any sunny day along San Francisco's Fisherman's Wharf, you can see young men standing immobile, statuelike, with mask-like faces, imitating the imitation. When they have to shift position, they do so with the clumsy, machinelike wobble of an eighteenth-century automaton. It is Turing's *imitation game* (page 159) played backward. If the man acts convincingly like a machine, has he then become a machine?

The act of imitation has undergone a profound transformation following the application of *digital* technology. The transcription of pictures and sound used to be accomplished by what we now call *analog* devices. The amount of silver deposited in a photograph was a measure of the brightness of the object at that spot. Taking a photograph of the photograph employed the same principle, but the reproduction was never perfect. It is inherent in most any analog copying process that the copy is never as good as the original.[9] Hence, as one proceeds to make copies of the copies, the image would progressively deteriorate. The same is true in the analog reproduction of sound if rerecorded on standard tape.

Digital reproduction works differently. The brightness of a spot on the image, or the loudness and pitch of sound on a record, no longer vary continuously from one extreme to the other, but are encoded as binary numbers, that is, series of digits like zeros and ones or *on* and *off*. Copying the record or image involves placing a *zero* for every *zero* and a *one* for every *one* encountered. This can be done, for all practical purposes, without errors. Hence the copy is no longer an *imitation* of the original. It is *every bit* as good as the original. Furthermore, copying can be done inexpensively, instantaneously, with the push of a button.

This new technology has put a severe strain on attempts to protect intellectual property. Anyone can make a perfect copy of valuable information, software, books inscribed digitally on *floppy disks*, making a mockery of copyright laws. In a feeble attempt to protect their property, "the *Software Publishers Association* has begun a campaign in schools that includes a rap music video entitled 'Don't Copy That Floppy.' "[10]

Our "pleasure of imitation" has often had as its goal the copying of that most complex object of all: our self. We have cited, in chapter 4, the crude attempts of the eighteenth-century French mechanists and—in this chapter—the more sophisticated efforts of Disney's audio-animatronics. But it was the advent of the modern high-speed digital computer that suggested we tackle the ultimate task: imitation of the human mind.

We have touched several times on the subject of artificial intelligence. The question of whether we can make a device that is able to duplicate the qualities of mind is still unanswered.

I have devoted much of this volume to presenting the proposition that a simple neural mechanism that I have called the *creative loop* can imitate objects by creating mental images and thus provide the raw material for imagination and creativity. But mechanisms can be duplicated, which would suggest that thinking machines should soon be within the realm of our technology. We certainly should be able to incorporate the kind of feature-enhancing feedback loops described in chapters 8 through 10 in a computer program or hardware device. In fact, we did that in the many computer simulation tests of the proposed process (see pages 86–87 and the appendix).

Have we achieved the aim of artificial intelligence? I think not. The mechanism appears on the surface to conform to the materialist notion of a machine that operates with clocklike precision. It is, however, no ordinary machine. The amplifying characteristic of the feedback loops, the *zoomability* as it was called, make the mechanism inherently nonlinear (see note 17 of chapter 13). This gives the brain the capacity for bootstrap processes, to make something out of virtually nothing using the ever-present noise as the source of its unpredictability. In processes that are likely to involve chaos, these minute fluctuations become selected and amplified until they become macroscopic phenomena.

Of course, the introduction of randomness and chaos alone are not what distinguishes the brain from a machine. A roulette wheel has both. The real difference is that in the brain the source of unpredictability is not *random* noise, but a noise that contains fragments collected over a lifetime, like a sediment rich in fossils, both large and small. The wealth and complexity of this treasure are beyond description. It is doubtful that they could ever be reproduced in all detail. The creative loops in our brain are tuned to these voices and whispers of the past, from which they compose the images and thoughts of the present.

Our "simple mechanism" thus is linked to processes that appear far from mechanistic. The picture of the brain operating like a machine is at best only part of the story, and we cannot claim with any kind of assurance that a machine will someday achieve brainlike attributes. This demechanization of brain function is only one aspect of a general change in our interpretation of nature. The picture of matter made up of hard and permanent particles that has formed the basis of our scientific outlook for so long has been abandoned in contemporary physics. Exploration of nature has been pushed far below the level of the smallest particles, and what is revealed there bears no resemblance to classical concepts of material. In a highly readable book entitled *The Matter Myth*, two physicists, Paul Davies and John Gribbin, write:

> *Many people have rejected scientific values because they regard materialism as a sterile and bleak philosophy, which reduces human beings to automatons and leaves no room for free will and creativity. These people can take heart: materialism is dead.*[11]

The book ends with this sentence: "Today, on the brink of the twenty-first century, we can see that Ryle was right to dismiss the notion of the ghost in the machine—not because there is no ghost, but because there is no machine."

〽〽〽〽

It is still intriguing to ask the question "What if?" *What if* our engineers succeed in constructing a truly thinking computer? And what if, to complete the illusion, we could clothe it in an audio-animatronic body, making a perfect android, a human recreated in silicon hyperreality? Would it have been worth the effort? Certainly, there is value in the exercise, the challenge to our ingenuity. But the final product would be as useless as Vaucanson's duck. The ultimate kitsch! There are easier ways of making people and, anyway, there are too many of us already.

It helps to remind ourselves why machines were invented in the first place. Their real value lies not in their ability to mimic human qualities, but in doing for us the things humans are unable or unwilling to do. Their tasks should be *complementary* to our tasks, not *competitive*. A chess-playing computer is an interesting curiosity. Again, its value lies in the challenge and in the experience gained in building it. We may hope that—once a program succeeds in defeating the human world champion—the computer efforts can be directed toward other goals, and humans can go back and enjoy the game and competition among themselves.

We must guard against misuse of machine talent and against the myths some AI enthusiasts have spun around their creations. Our technology and the machines it produces are essential to human survival. Our well-being will depend on the vigorous pursuit of their steady improvement, which will engage the best of our ingenuity. They do *not* think, they do *not* feel pain, they have *no* ambition—not now, not in the foreseeable future, and possibly not ever, unless we want them to.

The ball, as politicians would put it, is still in our court. And since nobody (and no *thing*) is ready to do the thinking for us, this makes the postmodernist pronouncements all the more ominous. Are we really losing our intellectual grip?

The word we hear frequently in this connection is *bricolage*. It is derived from *bricole*, a term that in billiards means a shot that did not go as intended but was successful nevertheless: a haphazard, unmeditated, and hence undeserved achievement. Are we surviving not by our wits but by bricolage? We began part IV with Wallace Stevens's image of a woman "striding there alone" and with her song *making* the sea and the world. How different from the postmodernist image of a child, sitting by the edge of the sea, scratching figures in the sand.

The juxtaposition of the two images begs the question we raised at the beginning of the book: the relationship between the *I* and the *it*, the individual and the world, the self and the other. The theoretical physicist John Wheeler, commenting on this duality, speaks of an "*it from bit*,"[12] which I take to mean that the objects of the world attain their objective reality only through the subjective processing of information about them. It is through the *bits* of information that the multitude of *them* become woven into the fabric we call the universe.

This is no longer just a philosophical stance. Modern quantum physics has taught us that it is only through the action of an observer that the intrinsically statistical nature of physical systems is reduced to specific, unique states. Thus a photon passing through a double slit in a classical experiment performed by the Englishman Thomas Young in the beginning of the last century cannot be said to have gone through one slit *or* the other, but was in a *mixed state* unless and until a specific observation is carried out to distinguish between the two alternatives.

John Wheeler pointed out that this reality-producing effect of observation can even reach backward in time. Davies and Gribbin report a thought experiment in which an observation performed on light from a distant quasar could "affect the nature of that light—not just a few billionths of a second in the past, but *several billion years ago!*" They add that "the quantum nature of reality involves nonlocal effects that could in principle reach right across the Universe and stretch back eons of time."[13]

Thus, if we believe this interpretation of quantum mechanics, Wallace Stevens's image is closer to the truth. We see the creative loop at whose center we stand not just dipping into the murky microworld of noise and subatomic uncertainty, but also linking the individual to widening circles on a cosmic scale. It is man's conscious mind that removes locality from the laws of nature, assembles the otherwise dissembled world.

There is nothing metaphysical about this picture. What I have presented is a *physicalist* interpretation of mind and brain dynamics that differs radically from what is generally offered as *the* scientific—that is, the *materialist*—description. We are restored to a central position in the universe again because we are still—so far as anyone knows—the only intelligence (on earth and beyond) that inquires, observes, and understands nature. It is still true, as Protagoras said, that "man is the measure of all things, of those that are, that they are, and of those that are not, that they are not."

ᔕᔕᔕᔕ

What about postmodernist assessment of our present condition? I believe that it must be taken seriously, but need not be cause for despair. We see ourselves traveling through the dreary landscape of hyperreality, wandering through a hall of mirrors, and caught in the "vicious spiral of reflexivity." But the important thing is that *we see ourselves*, which is precisely why I think that we will go on, and civilization will go on, and humanity will remain in charge for some time to come. Evolution has made us creatures of habit, looking for an adaptive niche and staying there. But what distinguishes us from the rest of the animal kingdom is our ability to break out of the trap when it threatens to become a dead end. We may languish for a while in the comfortable niche of intellectual stagnation until the glint of a distant reflection brings home the full impact of our predicament, our foolishness. Hope, finally, lies not in the denial of hopelessness but in our perception of it.

Appendix

Hill Climbing and the Optimization Problem

Imagine that you are wandering in a strange landscape and you are trying to reach the highest point in the area. To make matters worse, you are enveloped in a thick fog, making it impossible to see the terrain in front of you. You have only one aid: a very accurate altimeter that tells you after every step you take whether you have gone up or down. How will you proceed?

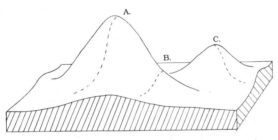

Attempts at hill climbing. Paths may lead to a major peak (A), a ridge (B), or a minor peak (C).

Chances are, you will take a trial step in a random direction. If you find that your altimeter told you that you have lost height, you probably will go back and move in the opposite direction. If you have gained height, you probably will continue in the same direction. Sooner or later your altimeter will tell you that you are no longer climbing. Perhaps there will be no change for a few steps, and then you find that you are losing altitude again. If you are very lucky, you will have reached the peak (*A*) that you were seeking. However, chances are that you were merely crossing a ridge (*B*), going up on one side and down the other, but the peak is somewhere else. Or else you may have gone over a small hill, a secondary peak (*C*), not the big one you were looking for.

175

The problem is known to mathematicians as the *hill-climbing problem*. Many strategies, or *algorithms*, have been proposed, most involving some kind of trial-and-error procedure. The situation I have described is still relatively simple because the person is restricted to move in two dimensions. We speak of *hill-climbing in two dimensions*.

The problem can be generalized. Mathematicians, unlike ordinary people, have no difficulty imagining a space of more than three dimensions. Suppose you are operating a piece of machinery that has ten different control knobs. Turn one and it speeds up. Turn it some more and it slows down again. Turn another knob and the machine slows down, but when you turn it further it speeds up. Let us say that you want the machine to go as fast as possible. The trick is to find that combination of the settings of the ten knobs that gives you the highest speed. You now have a hill-climbing problem in ten dimensions, because there are ten *degrees of freedom*, that is, ten knobs. Some combination of settings will give you the best result, the peak of performance. This is why this problem is known also as an *optimization problem*.

The Alopex Optimization Algorithm

An optimization algorithm is a procedure to find the ideal setting of the ten knobs (or any number of such *control variables*) without knowing anything about the internal workings of the machine and what each of the controls does. The procedure is guided only by the value of the quantity that is to be optimized, in this case the speed of the machine—call it S.

The *Alopex* algorithm is a particularly effective way of achieving the optimal performance,[1] by adjusting the values of the control variables. It works in the following manner. In the problem cited above, let the settings of the ten knobs be given by the numbers x_1 through x_{10}, and let x_1^{old}, x_2^{old}, and so on be the last values these variables had. The Alopex algorithm now chooses the new settings to be

$$x_1^{new} = x_1^{old} + (random\ step) + (last\ change\ in\ x_1)(last\ change\ in\ S)$$

with similar expressions for variables 2 through 10.

Let me try to describe in words what is happening. Two terms are added to the old value of a given variable. One is a random step, which may be either up or down; the second is a product of two changes, the last change in x_1 and the last change in S. Suppose x_1 was increased in the preceding step, and let us assume that S also had increased. The product is therefore positive, and the last term in the above equation will add to the previous value of x_1. This may or may not push x_1 in the right direction, since S depends on all ten control variables. But it is somewhat more likely to be right than wrong. Over a number of trials, this contribution will outpace the random steps and will tend to maximize S.

Why add the *random* step to the previous value of x? It would seem that this could only mess things up. However, without it the procedure is likely to lead you only across a ridge (B) or to a secondary peak (C). The added noise is no guaranty, but it tends to shake you loose from ridges and minor peaks and greatly increases the probability of reaching the true peak (A).

The Picture-in-the-Head as an Optimization Problem

I described in chapter 9 my supposition that images can be drawn at peripheral sensory centers by feedback from above. The pattern to be generated is to be that which—by virtue of being anticipated—produces the strongest response in some cortical *feature extractors*. This is shown schematically in the diagram below. Here a screen is made up of many pixels, each controlled by the optimizer (A).

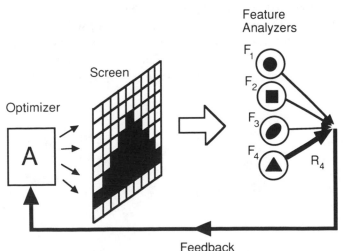

The Alopex optimizer (A) *enhancing the pattern of a triangle detected by an analyzer in the brain.*

The pattern that appears on the screen is observed by a number of feature analyzers, F_1, F_2, and so on. Each of these is sensitive to a particular feature indicated here schematically. F_1 is designed to detect circles, F_2 squares, F_3 ellipses, and F_4 triangles. F_4 therefore will have a strong response, R_4, when a triangle, or something resembling a triangle, appears on the screen. The optimizer will now function to maximize that response by adjusting the pixel intensities on the screen to make the pattern even more like a triangle. The pixel intensities are here like the control knobs in the example of the machine above.

❀❀❀❀

I mentioned (page 82) that producing the mental image is like inverting the sensory process. The optimization algorithm provides the kind of top-down control by which this can by accomplished. I have shown also[2] that the neural mechanisms by which something like the Alopex algorithms are to be enacted are extremely simple, and are readily performed by neural circuitry known to exist, for example, in the LGN.

One other feature of the mechanism is important here. Suppose the pattern on the screen is initially random, resembling none of the features recognized by the analyzers. As a result, the optimizer will get only faint responses from the various analyzers. The pattern on the screen is changing continuously due to noise. When a fluctuation makes the pattern resemble a triangle more than a circle, or a square, or an ellipse, the triangle-response R_4 begins to dominate in the feedback, and the optimizer will make the pattern on the screen become more like a triangle. The system has thus *selected*. It is this *nonlinear* feature that provides the all-important self-referent characteristic that initiates the bootstrap mechanism.

Notes

Preface

1. In *high-energy physics*, powerful accelerators are used to explore a world many times smaller than the nucleus of an atom. The enormous concentrations of energy created by the impact of speeding particles are beginning to approach conditions that must have prevailed soon after the origin of the universe in the so-called *big bang*. This brings together cosmology and the studies of the ultrasmall.

Introduction

1. Here, and throughout the book, *man* refers to an individual of the species *homo sapiens*, with no gender distinction intended. It is unfortunate that in the English language the only gender-free equivalent to the German *mensch* is the awkward *human being* or its shortened form, *human*. Likewise, the personal pronouns force the writer to select between *he* and *she* when referring to any person.

2. D. C. Dennett, 1991.

3. R. Penrose, 1989.

4. G. M. Edelman, 1992.

5. O. J. Flanagan, Jr. 1992.

6. J. R. Searle, 1992.

7. I discussed this point at length in a previous book (Harth, 1990).

8. Camille Paglia, 1990, p. 38.

9. One such theory, called *directed panspermia*, was proposed by Francis Crick (1981).

10. P. Davies and J. Gribbin, 1992.

11. O. B. Hardison, 1989.

Chapter 1

1. The account here is frankly limited to the perspective of Western civilization. Lively activity in the natural sciences preceded the Copernican revolution in other cultures.

2. Sir Francis Bacon, 1606.

3. A. Einstein, "On the Generalized Theory of Relativity," *Scientific American 182*, 1-6, 1950.

4. Ibid.

Chapter 2

1. E. Jantsch, 1981.
2. This quotation by John Wheeler is taken from Barrow and Tipler (1986).
3. H. Pagels, 1986.

Chapter 3

1. R. C. Lewontin, "The Science of Metamorphoses," *New York Review*, April 27, 1989.
2. C. de Duve, "Prelude to a Cell," *The Sciences*, Nov./Dec. 1990.
3. K. Lorenz, 1987, p. 21.

Chapter 4

1. R. Kearney, 1988.
2. L. Boltzmann, 1974.
3. K. Capek, 1923.

Chapter 5

1. The quotations are from W. S. McCulloch and W. H. Pitts, "A Logical Calculus of Ideas Immanent in Nervous Activity." This article and the later "Why the Mind Is in the Head" are included in the collection of works by McCulloch (1965).
2. G. Sarton, 1952.

Chapter 6

1. For more detailed information on this nonsynaptic information flow, see, for example, Fuxe and Agnati (1991).
2. The paper, McCulloch and Pitts, "A Logical Calculus of Ideas Immanent in Nervous Activity," *Bulletin of Mathematical Biophysics 5*, 115–133, 1943, is reprinted in an anthology (McCulloch, 1965).
3. F. Rosenblatt, 1962.
4. M. Minsky and S. Papert, 1969.
5. The literature on artificial neural networks is vast, including the work I carried out with my students in the 1960s and 1970s (see, for example, *Biophysical Journal 7*, 689, 1967; *Journal of Theoretical Biology 26*, 93 and 121, 1970; also *40*, 77, 1973).

Chapter 7

1. S. Zeki, "The Visual Image in Mind and Brain," *Scientific American*, Sept. 1992.

2. D. C. Dennett, 1991, p. 111.

3. A. R. Damasio, in peer review of D. C. Dennett and M. Kinsbourne, "Time and the Observer: The Where and When of Consciousness," *Behavior and Brain Sciences 15*, 208, 1992.

4. See, for example, D. Marr and T. Poggio, "From Understanding Computation to Understanding Neural Circuitry," *Neuroscience Research Progress Bulletin 15*, 470, 1976; also D. Marr, 1982.

5. R. M. Restak, 1979.

Chapter 8

1. The beginnings of the theory outlined here were first presented in 1976 (E. Harth, *Biological Cybernetics 22*, 169–180).

2. Napoleon is standing between the two trees on the left.

3. J. A. Hobson, 1988.

4. D. Dennett, 1991, p. 126.

5. B. Russell, 1927.

6. S. M. Kosslyn, 1983, p. 72.

7. R. N. Shepard and J. Metzler, "Mental Rotation of Three-Dimensional Objects," *Science 171*, 701–703, 1971; R. N. Shepard and L. A. Cooper, 1982; L. A. Cooper and R. N. Shepard, "Turning Something Over in the Mind," *Scientific American 251*, 106–114, 1984.

8. S. M. Kosslyn, T. M. Ball, and B. J. Reiser, "Visual Images Preserve Metric Spatial Information: Evidence from Studies of Image Scanning," *Journal of Experimental Psychology: Human Perception and Performance 4*, 47–60, 1978.

9. J. E. Pfeiffer, 1982.

Chapter 9

1. L. A. Cooper, and R. N. Shepard, "Turning Something Over in the Mind," *Scientific American 251*, 106, 1984.

2. A discussion of this can be found in R. N. Haber's article, "The Impending Demise of the Icon" and peer commentary, *Behavioral and Brain Sciences 6*, 1–54, 1983.

3. S. M. Kosslyn, 1980.

4. D. C. Dennett, 1991.

5. L. Rothblatt and K. H. Pribram, "Selective Attention: Input Filter or Response Selection?," *Brain Research 39*, 427, 1972.

6. J. C. Eccles (1989) finds it more persuasive to invoke a nonphysical *mind* that acts on the physical neurons by way of what he calls *psychons*.

7. Conjectures on the role of the feedback pathways go back many years. In 1950 E. van Holst and H. Mittelstaedt talked about the *principle of reafference* (*Naturwissenschaften 37*, 464, 1950). Later L. Rothblatt and K. H. Pribram suggested that the LGN act as a filter that can select incoming stimuli (*Brain Research 39*, 424, 1972). F. H. C. Crick similarly proposed a *searchlight hypothesis* that had the LGN direct attention toward specific features in the input (*Proceedings of the National Academy of Sciences 22*, 4586, 1984).

8. E. Harth, "Visual Perception," *Biological Cybernetics 22*, 169, 1976.

9. E. Harth, K. P. Unnikrishnan, and A. S. Pandya, "The Inversion of Sensory Processing by Feedback Pathways," *Science 237*, 184, 1987; E. Harth, A. S. Pandya, and K. P. Unnikrishnan, "Optimization of Cortical Responses by Feedback Modification of Sensory Afferents," *Concepts of Neuroscience 1*, 53, 1990; E. Harth, 1982.

10. D. Mumford, "On the Computational Architecture of the Neocortex," *Biological Cybernetics 65*, 135, 1991.

11. During the 1980s there was extensive research into what is called *implicit memory* (see, for example, S. Lewandowsky et al., 1989; also B. Bower, "Gone but Not Forgotten," *Science News 138*, 312–314, 1990.

Chapter 10

1. R. Penrose, 1989.

2. M. Stiles, E. Tzanakou, R. Michalak, K. P. Unnikrishnan, P. Goyal, and E. Harth, "Periodic and nonperiodic burst responses of frog retinal ganglion cells," *Experimental Neurology 88*, 176–197, 1985.

3. B. F. Skinner, "Selection by Consequences," *Science 213*, 501, 1981.

4. An excellent presentation of the subject for the general reader is J. Gleick's *Chaos*, 1987.

5. E. Harth, "Order and Chaos in Neural Systems," *IEEE Transactions on Systems, Man and Cybernetics 13*, 782, 1983.

6. H. Feigl, 1967.

Chapter 11

1. The term *zoomability* is attributed to George Reeke by Edelman (1989), p. 33.

2. G. M. Edelman, 1989, p. 67.

3. In the theory by the physicist Roger Penrose (1989, p. 438), many parallel and independent computations are simultaneously carried out at a *sub-quantum level* until one is selected that exceeds the *one-graviton threshold*.

4. D. C. Dennett, 1991, p. 274.

5. E. Harth, 1990, p. 123.

6. S. Faludi, "Speak for Yourself," *New York Times Magazine*, Jan. 26, 1992.

7. If the S-word jars you, its shock value is deliberate. But don't fret; it is only a word, like *mind* or *self*.

Chapter 12

1. For a discussion on the nature/nurture controversy, see, for example, Harth, 1990.

2. Self-reference as a factor beyond genetic and environmental influences that shape the individual was discussed in Harth, 1982 and 1990.

3. M. Minsky, 1985, p. 306.

4. N. Bohr, 1958, p. 97.

5. Dennett (1991) refers to E. M. Maruis's *The Soul of the White Ant*, Methuen, London, 1937.

6. M. S. Gazzaniga and J. E. LeDoux, 1970.

7. R. Puccetti, "The Case for Mental Duality," *Behavioral and Brain Sciences 4*, 93, 1981.

8. E. Harth, 1982.

9. D. MacKay, "Divided Brains—Divided Mind?" in Blakemore and Greenfield, 1987.

10. D. Parfit, "Divided Minds and the Nature of Persons," in Blakemore and Greenfield, 1987.

11. Ibid.

12. O. B. Hardison, Jr., 1989.

Chapter 13

1. G. Ryle, 1949.

2. B. Russell, 1959, p. 15.

3. D. Dennett, 1991.

4. M. Minsky, 1985.

5. In my usage the words *consciousness* and *awareness* are treated as synonyms.

6. E. Bisiach, "Understanding Consciousness," in Milner and Rugg, 1992, p. 113.

7. G. Edelman, 1989, p. 8.

8. L. Weiskrantz, 1986.

9. N. Humphrey, "The Inner Eye of Consciousness," in Blakemore and Greenfield, 1987.

10. G. Edelman, 1989, p. 69.

11. E. Harth, K. P. Unnikrishnan and A. S. Pandya, "The Inversion of Sensory Processing by Feedback Pathways: A Model of Visual Cognitive Functions," *Science 237*, 184, 1987.

12. F. Bacon, 1965, p. 81.

13. J.-F. Lyotard, 1991, p. 19.

14. N. Bohr, 1958, p. 8.

15. I have discussed this point in more detail in a paper entitled "Order and Chaos in Neural Systems: An Approach to the Dynamics of Higher Brain Functions," *IEEE Transactions SMC vol. 13*, 782–789, 1983.

16. M. Polanyi, quoted by Jeffrey Gray in Blakemore and Greenfield, 1987, p. 478.

17. When we say that a process is *linear*, we mean that the outcome depends *linearly* on any of the variables. Normal retail buying is a linear process: If we buy ten pounds of something, we pay ten times as much as we would for one pound. But sometimes this linearity breaks down. We may get wholesale rates if we buy more than a certain amount. A case of twelve bottles of wine costs less than twelve times the price of a single bottle. The process of buying wine becomes nonlinear for more than eleven bottles. In nature the appearance of nonlinear effects often makes computation of the outcome difficult, if not impossible. Chaos may occur. An extreme case of a nonlinear and chaotic process is the *butterfly effect* in meterology, mentioned in chapter 10.

18. F. Dyson, 1988, p. 295.

19. The instruction loop that generates the Mandelbrot set is simple: Take any complex number, call it c, square it, and add it to the original number. Call the result z. Next, take z, square it, and add c. Call the new result z. Continue indefinitely in this fashion. If the sum of the results of all these iterations remains finite, then the point represented by c is part of the *set*. The points belonging to the set represent the structure we call the *Mandelbrot set*.

20. J. Gleick, 1987, p. 231.

Chapter 14

1. D. C. Dennett, 1978, p. 124.

2. H. Gardner, 1985, p. 385.

3. E. Harth, "Does the Brain Compute?" *Behavioral and Brain Sciences 9*, 98, 1986.

4. A. M. Turing, "Computing Machinery and Intelligence," *Mind 59*, 433, 1950.

5. D. D. Swade, "Redeeming Charles Babbage's Mechanical Computer," *Scientific American*, Feb. 1993.

6. These and many other terms have been used by philosophers to describe the relationship between mind and brain. A good discussion of this can be found in Churchland, 1986. Very briefly, *substance dualism* holds that mind and brain are different substances, one physical, the other nonphysical. In *property dualism*, mental phenomena are considered as emerging from the physical brain without, however, being reducible to brain mechanisms. *Logical empiricists* believe in a unified structure and underlying logic in all sciences, including a science of the mind. Finally, in *epiphenomenalism*, the phenomena of sensation, consciousness, and other properties of mind are considered nonessential byproducts of the physical processes that constitute the brain's activities.

7. F. J. Dyson, 1988. See also an earlier technical article by Dyson, "Time Without End: Physics and Biology in an Open Universe," *Reviews of Modern Physics 51*, 447, 1949.

Chapter 15

1. The passages are from *After Truth: A Post-Modern Manifesto*, published by the 2nd of January Group, Inventions Press, London, 1986, as quoted by Kearney, 1988, p. 360.

2. J.-F. Lyotard, 1991, p. 203.

3. R. Kearney, 1988, p. 13.

4. U. Eco, 1986, p. 44.

5. R. Kearney, 1988, p. 341.

6. U. Eco, 1986, p. 46.

7. R. Kearney, 1988, p. 360.

8. O. B. Hardison, 1989, p. 326.

9. I discovered an interesting exception to this rule (E. Harth, B. Beek, G. Pertile, and F. Young, *Kybernetik 3*, 112, 1970). The phenomenon of lateral inhibitation in vision, discussed in chapter 7, gives rise to a stabilization of the image after the first few copies.

10. John Markoff, "In a World of Instant Copies, Who Pays for Original Works?," *New York Times*, 9 August 1992.

11. P. Davies and J. Gribbin, 1992, p. 13.

12. P. Davies and J. Gribbin, 1992, p. 307.

13. P. Davies and J. Gribbin, 1992, p. 214.

Appendix

1. The Alopex alogorithm was first proposed in 1974 (E. Harth and E. Tzanakou, *Vision Research 14*, 1475, 1974).

2. Harth, Unnikrishnan, and Pandya, *Science 237*, 184, 1987.

Bibliography

Sir Francis Bacon (1561–1626), "The Advancement of Learning" (1606), in *Francis Bacon: A Selection of His Works*, S. Warhaft (Ed.), Macmillan of Canada, 1965.

J. D. Barrow and F. J. Tipler, *The Anthropic Cosmological Principle*, Oxford University Press, New York, 1986.

C. Blakemore and S. Greenfield (Eds.), *Mindwaves*, Basil Blackwell, Oxford, 1987.

N. Bohr, *Atomic Physics and Human Knowledge*, Wiley, New York, 1958.

L. Boltzmann, *Theoretical Physics and Philosophical Problems*, D. Reidel Publ., Boston, 1974.

K. Capek, *R.U.R.*, Doubleday, New York, 1923.

P. S. Churchland, *Neurophilosophy*, MIT Press, Cambridge, 1986.

F. Crick, *Life Itself*, Simon and Schuster, New York, 1981.

P. Davies and J. Gribbin, *The Matter Myth*, Simon and Schuster, New York, 1992.

D. C. Dennett, *Brainstorms*, Bradford Books, Montgomery, Vt., 1978.

D. C. Dennett, *Consciousness Explained*, Little, Brown, Boston, 1991.

F. Dyson, *Infinite in All Directions*, Harper and Row, New York, 1988.

J. C. Eccles, *Evolution of the Brain: Creation of the Self*, Routledge, N.Y., 1989.

U. Eco, *Travels in Hyperreality*, Harcourt Brace Jovanovich, San Diego, 1986.

G. M. Edelman, *The Remembered Present: A Biological Theory*, Basic Books, New York, 1989.

G. M. Edelman, *Bright Air, Brilliant Fire*, Basic Books, New York, 1992.

H. Feigl, *The Mental and the Physical*, University of Minnesota Press, Minneapolis, 1967.

K. Fuxe and L. F. Agnati (Eds.), *Volume Transmission in the Brain*, Raven Press, New York, 1991.

H. Gardner, *The Mind's New Science*, Basic Books, New York, 1985.

M. S. Gazzaniga and J. E. LeDoux, *The Integrated Mind*, Appleton-Century-Crofts, New York, 1970.

J. Gleick, *Chaos*, Viking, New York, 1987.

O. B. Hardison, Jr., *Disappearing through the Skylight*, Viking, New York, 1989.

E. Harth, *Windows on the Mind*, Morrow, New York, 1982.

E. Harth, *Dawn of a Millennium*, Little, Brown, Boston, 1990.

S. W. Hawking, *A Brief History of Time*, Bantam Books, New York, 1988.

J. A. Hobson, *The Dreaming Brain*, Basic Books, New York, 1988.

E. Jantsch (Ed.), *The Evolutionary Vision*, AAAS, Westview Press, Boulder, Colo., 1981.

R. Kearney, *The Wake of Imagination*, University of Minnesota Press, Minneapolis, 1988.

S. M. Kosslyn, *Ghosts in the Mind's Machine*, W. W. Norton, New York, 1983.

S. M. Kosslyn, *Image and Mind*, Harvard University Press, Cambridge, 1980.

S. Lewandowsky, J. C. Dunn, and K. Kirsner (Eds.), *Implicit Memory*, L. Erlbaum, Hillsdale, N.Y., 1989.

K. Lorenz, *The Waning of Humaneness*, Little, Brown, Boston, 1987.

J.-F. Lyotard, *The Inhuman: Reflections on Time*, transl. by G. Bennington and R. Bowlby, Stanford University Press, Stanford, 1991.

D. Marr, *Vision*, Freeman, San Francisco, 1982.

W. S. McCulloch, *Embodiments of Mind*, MIT Press, Cambridge, 1965.

A. D. Milner and M. D. Rugg (Eds.), *The Neurophysiology of Consciousness*, Academic Press, San Diego, 1992.

M. Minsky, *The Society of Mind*, Simon and Schuster, New York, 1985.

M. Minsky and S. Papert, *Perceptrons*, MIT Press, Cambridge, 1969.

J. Monod, *Chance and Necessity*, Knopf, New York, 1971.

J. v. Neumann, *The Computer and the Brain*, Yale University Press, New Haven, 1958.

H. Pagels, *Perfect Symmetry*, Bantam Books, New York, 1986.

C. Paglia, *Sexual Personae*, Yale University Press, London and New Haven, 1990.

R. Penrose, *The Emperor's New Mind*, Oxford University Press, New York, 1989.

J. E. Pfeiffer, *Creative Explosion*, Harper and Row, New York, 1982.

F. Ratliff, *Mach Bands*, Holden-Day, San Francisco, 1965.

R. M. Restak, *The Brain: The Last Frontier*, Doubleday, Garden City, N.Y., 1979.

F. Rosenblatt, *Principles of Neurodynamics*, Spartan Books, New York, 1962.

B. Russell, *The Analysis of Matter*, Allen and Unwin, London, 1927.

B. Russell, *My Philosophical Development*, Allen and Unwin, London, 1959.

G. Ryle, *The Concept of Mind*, Hutchinson, London, 1949.

G. Sarton, *A History of Science*, Harvard University Press, Cambridge, 1952.

J. R. Searle, *The Rediscovery of Mind*, MIT Press, Cambridge, 1992.

R. N. Shepard and L. A. Cooper, *Mental Images and Their Transformations*, MIT Press, Cambridge, 1982.

L. Weiskrantz, *Blindsight: A Case Study and Implications*, Clarendon Press, Oxford, 1986.

Index